Saved without Swords

Saved without Swords

Who Can Be Saved, and How?

WILMA ZALABAK

WIPF & STOCK · Eugene, Oregon

SAVED WITHOUT SWORDS
Who Can Be Saved, and How?

Copyright © 2022 Wilma Zalabak. All rights reserved. Except for brief quotations in critical publications or reviews, no part of this book may be reproduced in any manner without prior written permission from the publisher. Write: Permissions, Wipf and Stock Publishers, 199 W. 8th Ave., Suite 3, Eugene, OR 97401.

Wipf & Stock
An Imprint of Wipf and Stock Publishers
199 W. 8th Ave., Suite 3
Eugene, OR 97401

www.wipfandstock.com

PAPERBACK ISBN: 978-1-6667-5963-1
HARDCOVER ISBN: 978-1-6667-5964-8
EBOOK ISBN: 978-1-6667-5965-5

12/22/22

Bible selections are from New Revised Standard Version Bible, copyright © 1989 the Division of Christian Education of the National Council of the Churches of Christ in the United States of America. Used by permission. All rights reserved.

Some Bible passages are paraphrased by the author of this book, either to summarize and shorten the quotation substantially or to update the tone and vernacular for a character in conversation. Any such paraphrases are so marked.

Dedicated to Bible re-readers everywhere.

Contents

Introduction		ix
1	Old Testament Stories: Saved without Swords	1
2	Luke: Jesus Saves	16
3	Romans: Who Can Be Saved, and How?	59
Bibliography		101

Introduction

Each chapter of this book is made of material I preached for Lent. Lent is the time of the church year in which we are encouraged to do introspection and confession. Lent precedes and leads up to Easter. Another excellent time to use this book is during the lead-in to Thanksgiving in preparation for the Advent season.

The Old Testament stories came out of preaching on the street in 2016. These are shorter than the other pieces which were preached in First Christian Church (Disciples of Christ) in Marietta, Georgia. Romans came during the first wave of COVID-19, in 2020, and Luke during COVID-19 recovery in 2022.

I left in this copy some evidences of its first presentation, some incomplete sentences, the use of the 1989 edition of the New Revised Standard Version of the Bible, and some work with the COVID-19 pandemic which took over our lives during this time.

I believe Lent and the humility before God that is taught by the Bible readings recommended for Lent, are prime contexts in which to get wise regarding our own lack of control, power, and superiority, as well as our persistent desire to claim these for ourselves.

In chapter 1, "Old Testament Stories: Saved without Swords," we will consider some very unfair situations with smart bullies and large tormentors. Rather than nurturing resentment and revenge, we will consider what Bible story characters did in similar

INTRODUCTION

circumstances. Our confession will be that we did not trust enough in God's ways, and now we can do better at that.

In chapter 2, "Luke: Jesus Saves," we will rejoice in Jesus' deliverance and come face-to-face with the one lesson Jesus longed to know that we had learned. We will follow Jesus, alone and in the crowds, to learn his deepest desire for our good and his strongest lament. Our confession will be that, more than anything else, we need Jesus.

In chapter 3, "Romans: Who Can Be Saved, and How?," we will don our logic hats and follow Paul's reasoning about being saved. We have gleaned hints about what it is from which we will be saved, and Paul spells it out, with many metaphors and in various ways. Our confession will be that our purpose on earth, in Christ, is to be freed from shame and to be a blessing to others.

For the purposes of this book, the word "saved" may have any or all of a wide variety of meanings. Many of us assign it a theological meaning, for instance, "saved from sin" and "saved to serve." It is linguistically appropriate to overlay that meaning with many other more mundane meanings. With the following list of synonyms and near-synonyms, would you ponder and circle the words that reach out to you in specific ways, and note, for each word you marked, what it is from which the fulfilling of that word would save you? Here are the words: defended, delivered, disentangled, emancipated, extricated, forgiven, freed, guarded, liberated, pardoned, preserved, protected, reclaimed, recovered, redeemed, reformed, released, rescued, restored, retrieved, safeguarded, salvaged, shielded, supported, sustained.[1]

The thoughts given here, whichever prove helpful, are called into existence by the God who knows the end from the beginning, and who can free us from pandemics, both COVID-19 and fear, shame, and guilt.

---

1. "Saved," *Merriam Webster Thesaurus*.

1
Old Testament Stories

Saved without Swords

GRASSHOPPERS AND HORNETS, NUM 13:1—14:12

What is bothering you right now? What is holding you back from your dreams? What unfairness seems to follow your footsteps?

Well, these Bible stories might make a difference for you. Come along with me. I promise you it will be a journey worth taking. Here is a map (drawn not so accurately by me) showing the tribes and empires we will meet in this journey.

Map of Rome to Babylon

First, please observe with me a couple of insects.

The people were ready, half a million people poised to go home. The advance intelligence about their new home was that it was beautifully situated, fruitful, productive, and already effectively supporting human habitation. Twelve people had gone there to gather this information, and two of them produced a moving inspirational presentation. "Let's go!" they said.

One might think the crowd would be unstoppable in moving out, but not so.

Ten of the intelligence crew, more than 80 percent of them, wailed and moaned and grumbled and spread fear throughout the crowd. Among other statements, they cried out, "We are like grasshoppers beside the giants of that place!" (Num 13:33, author paraphrase).

Grasshoppers!

"As grasshoppers, we'll get stepped on, pushed aside, and hated. We'll only go there to die! Oh, no! We must return to where we knew what our death would look like!"

The crowd rose up and rioted, turning their faces away from the adventure toward which they had been traveling for a more than a year. They turned back, and the inspiration of the two had no power to sway them toward trusting God again and going forward.

Grasshoppers. "To ourselves [and to them] we seemed like grasshoppers" (Num 13:33).

However, in the Bible, grasshoppers have an additional metaphorical meaning besides smallness. In a story we will read here later, the enemy armies came in like grasshoppers, eating as they came, and covering the ground (Judg 6:5; 7:12). Had the ten advance intelligence officers been able to turn around the grasshoppers metaphor, into adventure rather than fear, they would have known that God would make a way for them to enter their new home.

Grasshoppers are not the only insects used as metaphors. In God's instructions for Israel's entrance to their new home, God said he would send hornets to make a way for them. The meaning of the Hebrew word translated "hornets" is not very clear and might simply mean the trouble and terror that God would use to keep any enemies from hindering them (Exod 23:27–30; Deut 7:20–23, see footnote).

At any rate, there are scholars who believe that it was not God's plan to have people fighting any wars, but that God would make a way for them without swords. This series of stories from the Old Testament features people being *saved without swords,* some instances where the trouble was handled without fighting and people were enabled to thrive despite the odds.

Please ponder and talk with God about your current enemy or difficulty (or that facing your church, family, business, or ministry). Name it. Describe its history in your life. Name all pieces (even financial pieces) of what it is stealing from you. Imagine some ways God could handle the situation without your fighting. Name what you are afraid of happening if you did decide to refuse to fight and step firmly into believing in God's power to save. Describe, and in your imagination let yourself feel now and often, how you will feel when God has handled the situation.

Let's go!

Saved without Swords

MOSES, EXOD 14:1-31

After all, the people were slaves. They were not outdoors people. They had taken no wilderness survival classes. Obviously, they had gotten lost in the wild deserts.

Except this was Israel, and God was with them! God gave them air conditioning during the day and special effects lighting at night.

Pharoah came after them, expecting an easy capture, expecting them to be hot and despairing, lost and ready to fall into his hands, begging to be taken back to the comforts of home. He was mistaken.

Moses said to the people of Israel, "Do not be afraid, stand firm, and see the deliverance that the Lord will accomplish for you today; for the Egyptians whom you see today you shall never see again. The Lord will fight for you, and you have only to keep still" (Exod 14:13-14).

Egypt has a long history, and the interactions of Israel's ancestors with Egypt had mixed reviews. Abraham found shelter there from famine, irritated the Pharaoh with his half-truths, and was expelled (Gen 12:10-20). Jacob also found shelter there and sustenance during a great famine because Joseph had been sent on ahead and was blessedly enabled to offer them a royal welcome there (Gen 46:1-7; 47:1-12). Yet over hundreds of years, the welcome in Egypt deteriorated drastically.

The Egyptians mentioned here were Israel's former bosses, supervisors, and drivers, their former owners. The people of Israel had absorbed the view of themselves put upon them by the people with the power, tools, and willingness to hurt them. They were unarmed, unthinking, incompetent, and had no goals for themselves. The Egyptian slave drivers were cunning and cruel, imposing and insistent.

Who could resist Pharoah and his soldiers and slave masters? God could! "The Lord will fight for you, and you have only to keep still" (Exod 14:14).

The Lord used God's own climate and lighting systems to guide and protect Israel. This, however, did not get them over the primary obstacle. The sea blocked their way forward and the Egyptians were coming behind.

The Lord used Moses' walking stick and a strong east night wind to break through the huge barrier. Moses spread out his staff and the wind blew, and the water parted to reveal, in the light of the next day, dry ground on the sea bottom. Israel went over.

Let us review what Moses had told them. "Do not be afraid, stand firm, and see the deliverance that the Lord will accomplish for you today; for the Egyptians whom you see today you shall never see again. The Lord will fight for you, and you have only to keep still" (Exod 14:13–14).

Do not be afraid. Sometimes it is fear that stalls me. Worry and anxiety keep me stuttering on a decision. God says, "Don't."

Stand still, stand firm, and watch. Don't touch, just look. Don't just do something, stand there. Sometimes a forced inactivity produces the direst depression. Sometimes I pace, hunting for something I can do to fix a problem. God says, "Stand still and watch."

They did not really stand still, did they? Moving all possessions of a newly nomadic people even a mile would require huge expenditure of effort. They did not stand still. They walked through the sea. The way they needed to stand still was in not looking back. They had to determine to keep their minds facing front.

Sometimes I think of the last family moving through the sea. I wonder how many children they had, how many cattle, how many adults helping. I wonder if a child looked back in fear or even in excitement toward a sword-flashing battle. I wonder if the adults hurried a bit, close on the heels of the family who went before them.

Moses had said, "Do not be afraid, stand firm, and see the deliverance that the Lord will accomplish for you today; for the Egyptians whom you see today you shall never see again. The Lord will fight for you, and you have only to keep still" (Exod 14:13–14).

JOSHUA, JOSH 5:13—6:5

After Moses, God did have a succession plan. Joshua was to take over. Joshua had been the young assistant to Moses. After spending forty years in the desert learning to get along together, the tribes of Israel were now ready to enter Canaan, the place God had for them to live.

Joshua and Israel came first to Jericho, an ancient city situated in a beautiful oasis off the northwest coast of the Dead Sea. Biblical stories would lead us to believe that the entire Jordan valley was like one huge oasis at one time. Then Sodom denied the claims of God and reaped an unquenchable fire (Gen 19:1–29; compare Jude 7) that turned the whole valley into desert with one large basin of salt water and one fabulously beautiful oasis. I do not know whether people of Jericho had heard of Sodom and so built their city supposedly impregnable to the God of Israel. The fact that one family did turn to God and become part of the ancestry of Christ tells me that everyone there had an opportunity to choose God. Instead, Jericho shut its gates and placed its guards on the walls as Israel made its way to the home God had promised.

Joshua went out by himself where he could look at Jericho and there he prayed about how they were supposed to receive this at God's hand. The captain of the Lord's army appeared to him there and told him exactly how it was to be done.

Have all the people walk around the city once a day for six days, silently! Probably getting ready to go, marching, and coming back took a hunk of the morning. To someone in the crowd, it probably looked and felt like a lot of wasted energy just to go and be present for God around the city. Maybe that was time for any deserters from the city to make their way to a new God.

The captain explained further. On the seventh day have all the people walk around the city seven times, silently. On the seventh time around the city, have them all shout at once and let the trumpets blow. That is all.

You know what happened. The walls came tumbling down!

Would you have shouted? Do you think the effect had anything to do with the vibrations of the sound, albeit used by God? How well do you take care of your voice in order to shout for God? It is our voices that God wants to use in his battles. Near the end of our Bibles, we are told that God's people win against Satan "by the blood of the Lamb and by the word of their testimony" (Rev 12:11).

I think this makes it very important to take good care of our voices. (1) Do not shout, cough, clear the throat often, or talk much when sick. (2) Eat, exercise, and sleep well so all body functions can be at their best to support the voice. And (3) exercise your vocal cords by singing, yes, in the shower or the car alone if you think you cannot sing well enough for others to hear. Your speaking voice will have more pleasant resonance and resilience if you exercise your singing voice's full range. Just slide down the full range a few times every day.

The voice is a thing to cherish and train. God used human voices to bring down walls that were set against God's people.

The people were so full of themselves after the gain at Jericho that they went off with swords. They did! Without asking God for instructions, they strutted up to the little town of Ai, full ready now to do fantastic battle and heroic deeds. They got routed badly at Ai. There were no bragging campfire stories that night. Instead, they mourned thirty-six fallen soldiers and friends.

They had work to do with God. I suggest that God intended for Israel to gain the land without swords or fighting. God had already said he would use hornets to vacate the land for them (Exod 23:28; Deut 7:20), and Joshua would repeat that promise in his farewell speech (Josh 24:12). As mentioned earlier, the meaning of the Hebrew word translated "hornets" is not undeniably clear. It might include any number of other disasters or discomfitures. Yet, I guess the word "hornets" engages our imaginations well.

When has God held you back from violence and insisted you must use your voice while he used other means for your blessing?

GIDEON, JUDG 6:1-6; 7:1-23

They were hungry. All Israel was hungry. They hid in caves and mountain haunts to thresh and save a little grain.

The Midianites had discovered a source of free and abundant food. Midian was a son of Abraham and his second wife Keturah (Gen 25:2). Midian would have been step-uncle to Jacob who became known as Israel. Midian settled and grew on the eastern side of the Red Sea which was where Moses fled when he had to leave Egypt (Exod 2:15). The Midianites had been relatively hospitable to the Israelites as they journeyed from Egypt. Now however, when Israel was settled in its own land, they proved not so pleasant neighbors.

Every time the season came for Israel to plant or harvest, the Midianite armies would show up with tents and camels and other livestock, covering the ground as thick as grasshoppers. They would eat or destroy all the crops of Israel. The people tried to find secret ways to harvest. Still, they were hungry.

The people called on the Lord, and the Lord called Gideon, and Gideon put out a call for warriors. They came, thirty-two thousand of them to fight for their freedom and their families' food against multitudes without number of the Midianites.

The Lord said, "The troops with you are too many for me to give the Midianites into their hand. Israel would only take the credit away from me, saying, 'My own hand has delivered [saved] me.' Now therefore proclaim this in the hearing of the troops, 'Whoever is fearful and trembling, let him return home'" (Judg 6:2–3).

This was the law in Israel, that they should pronounce the invitation for anyone fearful to quit the army with no penalty and just go home (Deut 20:8). The difference in Gideon's story is that his army was so much smaller than what was needed, that he might not have sounded this invitation had God not insisted.

There was more to this than ridding the army of fearful liabilities. In this case, God insisted that Israel would take the credit toward the people away from God. Is this perhaps why God lets circumstances in our lives get worse before better, so that we will praise God and not our own prowess?

Well, twenty-two thousand left and ten thousand stayed at this first sort. The next sort left a mere three hundred warriors. God was pleased with this number.

The large camp of Midian and allies was below them in the valley. Gideon divided his men into three companies and gave every man a torch and a trumpet. With a torch in one hand needing to be steadied inside a clay jar to hide its light, and a trumpet in the other hand, no warrior had a hand free for a sword. That is why it was common in other battles for the commander or maybe a few others to carry the torch and the trumpet so the warriors could manage their swords and bows. Besides being few in number, these men were handicapped by what Gideon made them carry, with no hand available for offense or defense by sword.

Each of the three companies found a position on one of the hills surrounding the valley camp, and at one command, they broke the clay jars and blew the trumpets. No sword was needed. The enemy soldiers woke with a start, saw three hundred "commanders" on the hillsides, imagined how many swordsmen and bowmen there would be with each commander, and they killed each other in fright.

The record says, "Every man stood in his place all around the camp, and all the men in camp ran; they cried out and fled. When they blew the three hundred trumpets, the Lord set every man's sword against his fellow and against all the army; and the army fled" (Judg 7:21–22).

And the Lord got the glory.

ELISHA, 2 KGS 6:8—7:20

The ministry of Elisha was primarily in the northern part of Israel, long after the north-south split of the nation. Their capital was the city of Samaria. To Israel's north and east lay Aram, also called Syria, with its capital, Damascus.

Abraham had come from Aram. When he wanted a wife for his son Isaac, he sent to Aram to get one (Gen 25:20). When Isaac's son Jacob needed to get out of the house, he fled to his uncle Laban the Aramean (Gen 28:5). Centuries later, when there were kings in Israel, there was never any long-lasting peace between the kings of Israel and the kings of Aram.

Elisha's prophetic skills made him like a spy for Israel, as if placed intimately in the Aramean palace. The king of Aram kept sending out troops to raid various places in Israel. He began to notice that cities in Israel seemed to know plans made in the bedrooms of Aram. The king of Aram asked his advisors who the spy was.

They told him it was Elisha. Next, the king of Aram sent his armies with horses and chariots against Elisha. They surrounded the city of Dothan, where Elisha was staying. Elisha's assistant looked out a window and was shocked into fear by the sight of the number of soldiers all around the city.

Elisha said, "Do not be afraid, for there are more with us than there are with them" (2 Kgs 6:16). He asked God to open the eyes of his assistant who then saw horses and chariots of fire on the mountains surrounding both the city and the Aramean armies.

When Arameans on the horses and chariots got closer, Elisha prayed, "Strike this people, please, with blindness" (2 Kgs 6:18), and God did it! Elisha went out to them, asked them whom they wanted, and told them he would take them to the man they wanted. Elisha then led the Aramean armies to the palace of the king of Israel in Samaria, and once captured inside the city, he asked God to open their eyes.

The king of Israel said, "Shall I kill them? Let me kill them!"

Elisha said, "What? Kill those you just captured? No. Give them food and water and send them back to their king" (2 Kgs 6:21–22, author paraphrase). So that is what they did.

When Ben-Hadad was king of Aram, he brought his entire army against Samaria, the capital of Israel. The Aramean army settled in for a long siege against Samaria.

Inside the city, the famine became dire and created unacceptable conditions and inflation. The king of Israel was walking the city walls one day when a woman cried out to him for justice. This is how the king discovered that people were eating their own children to stay alive in the famine. This is when he decided to do go see Elisha.

Elisha said, "Here's what the Lord says: 'Tomorrow, about this time, food will be available for a small price at the gate of Samaria'" (2 Kgs 7:1, author paraphrase).

The scene changed to a spot just outside the wall of Samaria. There were four lepers, shut out from the city by their disease, and shut into this no-human-land by the armies encamped surrounding the city. The four lepers were starving. They sat there reasoning about things like worst case scenarios and how best to die. If they went into the city, they would die. If they stayed where they were, they would die. If they deserted to the Aramean camp, they could die, but they might find mercy and live. They went in the twilight to the camp, and they found the camp deserted!

What had happened was this. Shortly before the lepers decided to desert, the Arameans had heard sounds of a great army of horses and chariots and they reasoned that Israel had hired Hittite and Egyptian armies to come join the fight. The noise was so great and ominous that they all got up and ran pell-mell from the field, leaving all their tents, food, armor, treasures, and horses in place.

The four deserting Israelites ate and drank. They sat down in the first tent and satisfied their sharp-edged hunger. Then they spent some time gathering up silver and gold and good clothing and taking it to their cave. Then they decided to tell someone.

Understandably, the king of Israel worried that perhaps this was a trap; however, the intelligence crew he sent out came back with tales of a wild escape and all sorts of material thrown off along the way.

That afternoon food was cheap in Samaria, as Elisha had prophesied.

JEHOSHAPHAT, 2 CHR 20:1-30

"We treated them well and see how they repay us! They are bullies, much bigger and stronger than we are, and they pick a fight" (2 Chr 20:6-10, author paraphrase).

This is the story of what King Jehoshaphat did when Moab, Ammon, and Edom came to destroy Jerusalem. Moab and Ammon were the tribal descendants of two sons of Lot, born to him by his two daughters, after they fled from Sodom (Gen 19:36-37). Moab had been especially blamed when Israel was first entering Canaan because, with the help of an Aramean, Balaam, they first tried to curse Israel, and then they figured out how to bring down the curse of God on them by enticing them away from God (Num 22:7; compare Rev 2:14). The lands of Moab and Ammon flanked Israel on the eastern side of the Jordan River.

Saved without Swords

Edom was Esau's other name. Esau was the older twin brother of Jacob and the reason Jacob had to flee to Aram after he tricked Esau out of his birthright (Gen 32:3). The land of Edom lies to the south and east of Israel and Edom was very inhospitable to Israel on their journey into Canaan. Israel sent their king a respectful request to travel through their land on the highway (Num 20:14—21:4). Edom refused passage, causing Israel discouragement and a long march around their land to enter from the east of the Jordan near Jericho. Neither Edom, nor Moab, nor Ammon did the Lord allow Israel to harm on their way into Canaan (Deut 2). Now they got together to fight against Israel in its own land. What did the king do?

Before he made any military plans or strategies, King Jehoshaphat admitted that he was afraid, set himself to seek the Lord, proclaimed a fast throughout Israel, and supported the people's desires to assemble together to seek the Lord.

The king Jehoshaphat stood in the large assembly and talked straight to the Lord. He reminded the Lord that it was God who would not let Israel destroy Moab, Ammon, or Edom on their way to Canaan, and now the repayment for that good deed was punishment. Apparently, it is alright to complain openly to God about the unfairness of life.

"O our God," prayed King Jehoshaphat, "will you not execute judgment upon them? For we are powerless against this great multitude that is coming against us. We do not know what to do, but our eyes are on you" (2 Chr 20:12) Authenticity like this is part of wise leadership.

A prophet showed up and said, "Listen, all Judah and inhabitants of Jerusalem, and King Jehoshaphat: Thus says the Lord to you: 'Do not fear or be dismayed at this great multitude; for the battle is not yours but God's. Tomorrow, go down against them. . . . This battle is not for you to fight; take your position, stand still, and see the victory of the Lord on your behalf, O Judah and Jerusalem.' Do not fear or be dismayed; tomorrow go out against them, and the Lord will be with you" (2 Chr 20:15-17).

I think most people can keep from fighting if they do not attend the battle. However, this command was to attend but stand still. See the battle but do not be afraid. Go, but the battle is not for you to fight. Take your position, but the battle is not yours. This was a difficult command. I think this might be the most difficult command in all of biblical history. Stay present and engaged, but without worry or fight.

King Jehoshaphat said, "Believe in the Lord your God and you will be established" (2 Chr 20:20). King Jehoshaphat did more than just exhort them to believe. He took counsel with the people, and then he appointed singers to go out before the army.

Singers! I think Jehoshaphat knew this was a difficult task for the soldiers. That is why he created the strategy best suited to keep all those soldiers on track for believing God. He sent singers to move between the soldiers and the enemies.

The record is that when they started to sing and praise God, then Moab and Ammon attacked Edom and then each other. When Judah came upon the enemies, they were all dead corpses! Collecting the loot required three full days.

Especially in this story, I notice the unity of the people of Judah. When the king got authentic, and called them to join him in prayer, they came out for the event. They listened. They agreed to do the experiment together.

Sometimes might there be some people God wants to get to come together before God can pour out the needed victory?

HEZEKIAH, 2 KGS 18:28—19:37

The Lord brought Israel out of Egypt without swords. A few decades later, the Lord sent the swarming raiders called Midianites away from Israel, without swords. Then, about a thousand years before Jesus came, Israel became a great nation and a power reckoned among the other nations. David and Solomon passed into history and their kingdom split into northern and southern pieces. Elijah and Elisha prophesied in the northern kingdom. The Lord showed out a couple times for Elisha and his king, without swords. King Jehoshaphat ruled in the southern kingdom and saw the Lord drive away three long-time neighbors who had decided to join forces against Jerusalem, without swords.

Saved without Swords

Then there was Sennacherib, the ruthless king of Assyria. Assyria was a newcomer on the stage this far south, having its capital way north and east in Nineveh. Sennacherib had raided and destroyed all of the northern kingdom of Israel. He had burned their houses and fields and sent the people away to other lands. Now he was close to Jerusalem.

King Hezekiah sent to Sennacherib all the gold he could find, even scraping the gold plating off the walls of the temple. He begged Sennacherib to go away and leave Jerusalem alone. Sennacherib's response was to send his orator, Rabshakeh. He stood outside the gates and shouted his messages over and through the walls. He used the language of Judah. (I wonder how he came to know Hebrew.) Hezekiah's envoys asked him to speak in Aramaic so the people on the walls would not understand him and the message would be private for the king.

Rabshakeh spoke the more clearly in Hebrew saying he wanted the people on the wall to understand him. Then Rabshakeh began to mock Hezekiah and the God of Israel. He said, "Who among all the gods of the countries have delivered their countries out of my hand, that the Lord should deliver Jerusalem out of my hand?" (2 Kgs 18:35).

The people obeyed Hezekiah's command, and no one condescended to answer Rabshakeh. When King Hezekiah heard the words of Rabshakeh, he sent urgent word to Isaiah, the resident prophet at the time. He said, "This day is a day of distress, of rebuke, and of disgrace; children have come to the birth, and there is no strength to bring them forth" (2 Kgs 19:3).

Isaiah sent back this word from the Lord: "Do not be afraid because of the words that you have heard, with which the servants of the king of Assyria have reviled me. I myself will put a spirit in him, so that he shall hear a rumor and return to his own land; I will cause him to fall by the sword in his own land" (2 Kgs 19:6–7).

On the strength of that word from the Lord, Hezekiah and the people stood strong in faith through the next barrage of words and threats. Hezekiah took the letter with the mocking threats from Sennacherib into the temple, and there he prayed with extreme and urgent passion. "So now, O Lord our God, save us, I pray you, from his hand, so that all the kingdoms of the earth may know that you, O Lord, are God alone" (2 Kgs 19:19).

That night an angel from the Lord killed 185,000 soldiers of Sennacherib's army. The next morning there were only dead bodies on the field. Sennacherib left the area and went home to Nineveh. There he was killed by his sons while worshiping in the house of his god.

These are stories of when God's people were *saved without swords*. May we trust the Lord as effectively.

2

Luke

Jesus Saves

TEMPTATION'S "IF," LUKE 4:1-13

Luke's Storytelling

Who likes a story? Children like stories. Adults like stories in otherwise boring sermons! Preachers like stories; their voices modulate, their gestures relax, their urgency for decision takes a break until after the story. Everybody likes stories.

Luke liked stories. I have heard Luke described as an expert storyteller, and I have even tried to enter into contrary discussion with the person who asserted this. I have always seen Luke as the one who put Jesus in the role of superb storyteller. Matthew and Mark show Jesus telling stories, but Luke shapes those stories Jesus told into expert form. Luke shows Jesus as the superb storyteller, besides the compassionate healer, the respecter of the poor and the feminine in his audiences, and the accepter of the most sinful.

According to the first chapter of Luke, this Luke wrote after there were already Gospel stories or snippets or possibly full Gospels already circulating. That is about all we know about the date of writing. This Luke could have been the physician who traveled with Paul (Col 4:14). He could have been one of the close followers of Jesus through his ministry, though not chosen as one of the twelve. Indeed, this Luke could have been from later generations, having heard of Paul and the twelve and the stories and other written Gospels. I usually think in terms of the earliest possibilities; others choose later options.

This Luke, with both Luke and Acts from his pen, wrote more of the New Testament than even Paul did, and his language and style are more advanced and literary than any of the other New Testament writers.

I choose to agree with Fred Craddock, in his Bible commentary on Luke, where he characterizes Luke as an artistic preacher and not merely as a superb storyteller. To think of Luke as a preacher, we will observe two things. On the one hand, we will consider what is in front of us; we will attend "to the text of the Gospel as it comes to us."[1] Though we are aware that he drew from many sources, discovering his sources will not be our focus here. We will seek to hear what this Gospel says in the way it is laid out in our Bibles. Further, we will agree that it was written primarily to people who lived not long after the events of which it tells, and not written directly to us. We will keep the pieces in their written contexts while seeking to understand what the preacher Luke meant by his arrangement.

On the other hand, there are times that we will notice Luke's skill and techniques toward holding the attention of his audience and underlining his point. Fred Craddock lists some of these: "travelogues," "trials and courtroom scenes," "farewell speeches," "wonder stories," and "stories within the story." He adds, "Luke shows great skill in the use of contrasts" and "we can expect both to admire and to be captured by Luke's use of restraint so as to create anticipation. . . . Such restraint is a mark of an expert storyteller who knows how to capture and hold the participation of the listener."[2]

I would add that Luke was expert in flashback and flash forward. These two temporal skills, in that they have to do with

---

1. Craddock, *Luke*, 3–4.
2. Craddock, *Luke*, 6–7.

placement in time, often appear in literary artistry. So let us not be surprised when we have to discern the times, when the story is not necessarily presented as chronologically consecutive.

Between Hearing the Voice of God and Ministering to the People

Have you ever been in a situation where you felt the other person or persons were trying to keep you out late? My first hire as a minister was in a small church a long way from here. I pulled some very late nights. The members needed to talk, and I surely did hope I could get the husbands to come to church as their wives did. I visited and found myself sometimes unable to pull away until way past midnight. That certainly did not do my health any good. Then someone in one of the three families told me that they had a game among them to see which ones could keep me out the latest the most times. They were precious people, and I had no idea what to do with them. I have learned a little since then and I want to share some of that learning here.

The Bible portion for this chapter is in the introduction to the book of Luke. Here Jesus is fresh from the scene of his baptism, where he had heard his father's voice from heaven saying, "You are my Son, my Beloved. In you I am well pleased" (Luke 3:22). Jesus had listened carefully and taken it in. From what he heard, he knew he had family, purpose, and meaning. On the strength of that family, purpose, and meaning, Jesus went to the desert to pray. In the midst of his strong dedication to God, the devil came; however, he waited to come until after Jesus had fasted for six weeks and was weak and disfigured. This was the devil's chosen time to engage Jesus and see how long he could keep Jesus talking and distracted from praying.

"If You Are the Son of God"

Luke did not say from what direction the devil came, only that he started talking. Perhaps he was lurking, trying to overhear the prayers to God, watching for signs of breakdown, noting all the little things that could be buttons to push to get Jesus angry or defensive, and thereby more likely to make a mistake.

The devil said to him, "If you are the Son of God, command this stone to become a loaf of bread" (Luke 4:3).

You have heard it many times. "If you are a good mother, you will buy your children this swimwear or that robot-building kit." "If you were a good citizen, you would call your representatives." "If you were a good Christian, you would give me some money." "If you were a good church member, you would be here every time the doors open and a lot of time in between."

Suzette Haden Elgin wrote about verbal abuse and the defense against it. She identified the tone and content of abusive language that begins with "if." We will notice her principles in the language of the enemy of our Lord.[3]

You probably noticed, when you heard this kind of language, that there is usually some raising of pitch and decibels to get across the message. What is the message? First, the message is, "You should be ashamed, so that you will follow this conversation wherever and however long I make it run." Yet even shame is not the pivotal tool here.

There is the bait and the hook. The bait is what will keep you talking while the hook sinks deep. The bait is "you will buy your children this or that," and if you keep talking about brands and fashions, the hook will sink deep inside you persuading you that you are not a good mother. The bait is "call your representatives," which can keep you arguing while you absorb the information that you are not a good citizen. The bait is "be here every time the church is open," and while you calendar the next week's schedule as declared, or try to excuse yourself, you will take in the message that you are not a good church member and therefore ought to be ashamed of yourself.

Of course, Jesus was hungry! "If you are the Son of God, command this stone to become a loaf of bread," said the devil. The bait: "Make something to eat." The hook: "Surely you're not the Son of

---

[3] Elgin, *Gentle Art of Verbal Self-Defense*, 27–64.

God!" Another hook: "Look how thin and weak you are. You must be the OTHER son of God!"

Did Jesus parley with the bait? Hmmm. What kind of bread shall it be, wheat or white? Will there be fish with that?

No, Jesus went straight to the hook, the thing that was meant to seed doubt in his soul. He said, "It is written, 'One does not live by bread alone, but by every word that comes from the mouth of the Lord'" (Luke 4:4). That is a direct quotation from Deut 8:3. How does that deal with the hook, the snickering "If you are the son of God"? Jesus cited the last word from the mouth of God, which was, "You are my Son, my Beloved." Jesus destroyed the hook. He said in effect, "I am the Son of God because my Father says so. This is the word of God by which I live."

There was no room for temptation's "If" in Jesus' mind.

"If You Will Worship Me"

The devil showed Jesus all the kingdoms of the world with all the authority that goes with their ownership. "All these I will give you," said the devil. "If you, then, will worship me, it will all be yours" (Luke 4:6–7).

You have heard this one, too.

[The hook] "If only you would loan me $10, [the bait] I'll pay it back with interest next week." (Hmmm. How much could I make?)

[The hook] "If you'll just do it this once, [the bait] then you'll be one of us." (Hmmm. What might that mean?)

[The hook] "If you'll try this new street drug, do it for me, [the bait] we'll get stoned together and have a lot of fun." (Hmmm. Think of all the kinds of fun.)

[The hook] "If only you'd give me the director's position; [the bait] I'll get your family the choicest contracts." (Hmmm. I'm spending the extra money already in my thoughts.)

Jesus dallied not at all with the bait, the rich and dazzling cities, the wealth and authority and prestige he could have without going to the cross. He did not even argue with the devil about who really owned those kingdoms.

Jesus went straight to the hook and demolished it. "It is written," he said, 'Worship the Lord your God, and serve only him'" (Luke 4:8). Jesus allowed no time at all for that hook of worshiping the devil to settle in his mind and imagination.

How can I recognize verbal abuse? Often there is a prominent "if," maybe a "what if," maybe an "if only." There is always a "you" because that person wants to make it all about you, and never a two-way street. There is often some raising of the voice in volume or pitch, and if I raise my voice to match or exceed the other, well, that is how yelling matches get started.

Sometimes the verbal abuse comes from inside us, as if it were our own thoughts. Some of us have internalized the shame for so long that we can make it up for ourselves. "I ought to be able to talk to that person without yelling, if I'm a good Christian." "I should have gotten an A in that class, if I'm a good student." You might say, "But it is true, I ought to be ashamed." I said that. I did it long enough to learn that shame is not helpful. Even if I admit my shortfall, the shame and guilt connected with the "if" are not helpful.

Jesus knew immediately the trap introduced by the "if," and he shut it down. He used words from the Bible to shut the devil down, and I believe this will be our effective tool, too.

"If You Are the Son of God" Again

The devil took him to a high place and said, "If you are the Son of God, throw yourself down from here; hasn't God promised to catch you?" (Luke 4:9–11, author paraphrase).

If you really are the Son of God, then prove it, I dare you. If you really care about God's reputation, you'll give him a chance to show himself.

You have heard this in a myriad forms. "If you really cared about your children, country, church, the environment, the poor . . ." "If you really wanted to be promoted, to be healthy, to be kind . . ."

Jesus smashed the hook. He gave no thought to the bait: to the publicity to be gained by someone jumping to suicide and finding the fall interrupted half-way down. He ignored the bait: the idea of making God come at his own beck and call. He battled the hook. "It is written," he said, "'Do not put the Lord your God to the test'" (Luke 4:12).

I usually read this as Jesus saying something like, "My father is not to be tested, tempted, or dared." This time I read it as Jesus saying, "You know I am your Lord. The Bible says do not tempt your Lord." And that is when the devil left him.

The first thing and maybe the only necessary thing is to shackle the power of the hook. I can discuss the various issues brought up by the bait with some friend or therapist later. What I have to do is zap the hook, because if I take in the hook I will do things I had not decided on my own to do. I will take in the shame, and before long I will make the presuppositions of the hook sound like my own voice.

I can simply counter the hook. I can say it simply and say it again if necessary: "I am a good mother." "I care about the environment." "I want to be healthy." I will say it without the spikes in vocal volume and pitch. I will simply say it to myself, and others can overhear it. I am not ashamed.

I made it easy in this writing. I always put the "if" with the hook. Sometimes the "if" is not stated or is mixed in with the other. I have to look for what is it that this person wants me to do or think or feel. If I do not identify it, I will feel it anyway and it will shape other choices. Dealing with hooks mindfully takes time and practice.

Jesus' Weapon against the Hooks of Verbal Abuse

I must highlight here the most powerful weapon against verbal abuse hooks. Jesus used it every time, and it worked! Luke says the devil departed and waited for another opportune time. Jesus quoted the words of scripture, and somehow that stood up powerfully against the devil and his verbal abuse. It is never too late to start getting some of the word of God inside us, either by reading inductively for the big picture, or studying in depth one verse at a time, or memorizing selected passages. I am very pleased when I learn of prayer groups or discussion groups gathering to study the Bible. I believe this picture will yield great dividends for the church. Wycliffe Bible Translators tells this story:

> In an open area of a central Tanzanian community, hundreds of Burunge people gathered from miles around. It was time to celebrate. A procession of people came singing and dancing, carrying a box into the center of the gathering.
>
> As the crowd cheered, local church leaders and Bible translators opened the box to reveal the sweetest treasure the Burunge people could ever hope for—the New Testament in their language![4]

Jennifer Stasack tells another story for the Wycliffe Bible Translators:

> Toggle Owusu, the chief of Nyagbo-Sroe community [in Ghana], is an old man with an infectious, toothy smile and an enthusiasm for Bible translation work among his people. . . . The chief wants his people to be fed by God's Word—for every generation to be seated around the table.
>
> That is what Ghanaians are hoping and praying will happen. Their goal is to see their country changed by the Word of God.[5]

That is my goal for our country, my church, my life. Changed by the word of God, and not by temptation's "if."

I'M IN A GOOD YEAR, LUKE 4:14–21

Luke's Story So Far

As stated in the previous chapter, I choose to agree with Fred Craddock, in his Bible commentary on Luke, to characterize Luke as an artistic preacher. Luke arranged his Gospel with a clear beginning,

---

4. Wycliffe Bible Translators, *Frontlines*.
5. Stasack, "The Meal that Satisfies."

middle, and ending, in effective preaching modality. Luke made an A section, introduction, a B section, body, and a C section, conclusion. The A section runs from the first verse to Luke 9:50 and is where Luke spent time setting up the plot. Most of Jesus' work at this time was in Galilee, far to the north of Jerusalem. In the A section, the introduction to Luke, there are the birth and youth stories, John's ministry, and the genealogies, sort of crammed in at the beginning. Then there is careful set-up with forebodings of the conflict Jesus will have throughout his ministry, as he begins teaching, gaining renown, and choosing his disciples, there in Galilee.

Luke's B section is the development and complicating of the plot. He chose a common plot-organizing tool: a journey. Dante's *Divine Comedy* (1320) and Bunyan's *Pilgrim's Progress* (1678) both use the journey plot to teach concepts that might seem abstract or overwhelming if merely heaped all together. Luke's journey mode continues from Luke 9:51 to Luke 19:28 and effectively gets Jesus from Galilee to Jerusalem, though the journey cannot really be traced on a physical map from Galilee to Jerusalem. The journey is more in the readers' minds than on a map.

Luke's C section consists of the triumphal entry of Jesus into Jerusalem and all the events of the passion and resurrection. It runs from Luke 19:29 to the very last verse in the book, a dramatic conclusion to the tale and themes so well developed earlier. We will necessarily look at a small piece of Luke's plot in each chapter, and it will do us well to keep the larger plot in mind.

This time, we will work in the A section, the introduction. The setting for our reading is after Jesus' baptism by John, after the presentation of his genealogy, and after Jesus' visit to the wilderness, which occupied our last chapter. Our reading for this time is a beginning summary. Luke likes summaries, says Fred Craddock.[6] This one provides a sort of baseline for Jesus' ministry. He teaches in the synagogues and accumulates fame in the cities of Galilee.

Oops, he failed to go to Nazareth first! Would not a famous youth want his hometown to be his first stop? At least that is what his fellows and all the extra moms and dads in the village would

---

6. Craddock, *Luke*, 59.

think. Here we will study the first thing out of Jesus' mouth to his friends back home, the first thing out of Jesus' mouth in his whole ministry, as recorded by Luke.

We will review the bright picture given, and I will affirm for you that I'm in a good year. We can all take in Jesus' promise and find that we are in a good year. Because of Jesus, I'm in a good year.

To Bring, Preach, and Proclaim

The first words out of Jesus' mouth, according to the Gospel of Luke, comprise phrases from a rather lengthy quotation from Isa 61. You remember, all the Bible Jesus had was the Old Testament. It was the next thing to do for young men to visit a synagogue and be asked to read the scripture and comment on it.

A synagogue could be as small as ten adult males, and they gathered in not-so-formal meetings on the Sabbath. A young adult voice would almost certainly be called on. Jesus' fame had spread and reached back to his hometown. Now he came to the Nazareth synagogue and, of course, they gave him the scroll and asked him to read. The scroll was Isaiah.

Bible students that you are, what do you get when you compare Luke's account with the passage in Isaiah? I think this was the first reading I came across long ago from which I realized that things I expect to match do not always match in the Bible. There are some large differences here. My first solution was that Jesus must have been reading from the Greek translation of the Hebrew scriptures, and that is possible. It is also somewhat likely that he made his own translation or intentionally inserted the phrase about the blind seeing which was taken from Isa 42:7. This is one illustration of why we will not concern ourselves too much with sources in Luke. We will study the text as it stands now.

However, it is well to note that the origin of this saying is centuries before Jesus came on the scene in Nazareth. It was spoken by a messianic prophet to Israel in very difficult times. I say "messianic" because the word *messiah* in Hebrew, or *Christ* in Greek, translates to "anointed one," and this message, spoken by a prophet in hard times, includes a claim to be anointed. Jesus appropriated this reading to announce his anointing, his messiahship. "I've been anointed to preach good news, to proclaim release and recovery. And these are especially for the poor, the captives, and the blind" (Luke 4:18, author paraphrase).

There were some in the group who would quickly respond in thought, "I'm not bound. I'm not sick. Peddle your wares elsewhere, young man. I swaddled you when you were in diapers. I know a little about life." There were others who thought, "There's no one poor, captive, or blind here. I like the sound of your ministry, though. I always thought well of your momma. I hope you find those poor people to help them."

In a few minutes, we will explore where those internal responses led. For now, let us bask in Jesus' proclamations. Because of Jesus, I'm in a good year.

To Let the Oppressed Go Free

Those first three phrases of Jesus' statement were all in the realm of proclamation, preaching, and telling. Next, he added some action onto the words, and I think this action may include all of the previous phrases. Jesus is anointed to let the oppressed go free. He will set the poor free through his good news. He will set captives free and grant recovery of sight to the blind through his proclamations. He will let the oppressed go free.

I resonated with Mr. Jim Hill's story, of how he believed and told a young friend to get up out of the casket and live. That boy did not rise up, and Mr. Hill learned that he is not Jesus.[7] In the same way, I yearned to set free the poor, the captives, the blind, and the oppressed, and I have been working on that in various ways since my youth. I am slowly learning that I am not Jesus, and the first thing I can do to help anyone is to pray, and then to listen respectfully. Of myself, I cannot usher in the kingdom of no oppression.

Unlike me, Jesus was Jesus! He came to let the oppressed go free. My next question is, Why are not we all free? Why are there

---

7. Hill, "Every One of Us Has a Gift."

still oppressed people in this world? Why are there still the abused, the bullied, the trafficked, and the coerced? I am intense with God on this.

I have been reading Doris Kearns Goodwin's book about the presidents Theodore Roosevelt and William Taft, who came into leadership during the time when the results of industrialization were exploding in our nation.[8] On the one hand, if the presidents worked to break up or hinder big corporate trusts like Pullman, Standard Oil, and US Steel, then the people responsible for the prosperity of our nation could feel oppressed.[9] On the other hand, if the presidents turned a blind eye to bribes and rebates that put the small companies out of business in favor of the large companies, if they turned a deaf ear to the workers' complaints of low pay, dilapidated rental housing, long hours, and unsafe working conditions perpetrated by the large companies, then the poor certainly were being oppressed.[10] I thought as I read, "Most assuredly, I wonder how God would make equity here."

As I work at it and get an oppressed person freed, do I not in that act "oppress" the ones who have chosen the role of oppressor, probably trying by these means to survive their own oppressions? Who oppresses except those who have been oppressed? Fairness for all is not at all a clear call. The ponderings and puzzles abound.

Also, someone mentions the oppressions produced when the poor, the captives, and the blind somehow get their statuses reversed. The people could feel oppressed who must bear the economic losses, in interest on loans, in jobs in the welfare system, in cheap labor for the ugly jobs, and in wealthy donations to political campaigns. Besides that, what if some of those who appear to be oppressors really are, also, in some way poor, captive, blind, and currently oppressed? Though I can work for the oppressed person in front of me, I cannot fathom how to fix all these oppressions in justice for everyone on all sides. I am not Jesus.

Yet I do say, Because of Jesus, I'm in a good year!

8. Goodwin, *Bully Pulpit*, 158-433.
9. Goodwin, *Bully Pulpit*, 158, 254, 295, 299.
10. Goodwin, *Bully Pulpit*, 356-357.

SAVED WITHOUT SWORDS

To Proclaim the Year of the Lord's Favor

The fifth and last line that Jesus used in quoting from Isaiah to proclaim his anointing, his messiahship, claims that this is the year of the Lord's favor. Jesus declared this the year. Jesus proclaimed, "This is the year of God's blessing."

You say, "That was back then."

Indeed, and back then Jesus inaugurated a new kind of government, a continuing, yearly year of the Lord's favor.

Yet there is still oppression. There are still the abused, the bullied, the trafficked, and the coerced. People with strong ideologies have tried for centuries to rid the world of oppression. Now we are in the midst of a huge human effort to bring the world around to utopia by sustainable development goals[11] concerned not only with climate but also with undoing oppressions. Many people feel you cannot undo oppressions without creating or ignoring other oppressions. I believe only Jesus can let the oppressed go free fairly and sufficiently. He did it when he was here. Indeed, he did it though I cannot see it. We are already free now in this year of the Lord's favor, and we look forward with eagerness to God's great reset when God himself ushers in touchable righteousness on earth.

The question is, Will I believe Jesus' word that this is the year of the Lord's favor?

If I catch a cold from giving away my socks as Mr. Hill did,[12] will I still affirm Jesus' proclamation that this is the year of the Lord's favor? If my house gets flooded, will I still affirm Jesus' proclamation that this is the year of the Lord's favor? If my friends die, or even if I die, of COVID-19, will I still affirm Jesus' proclamation that this is the year of the Lord's favor? If our attendance numbers drop at church, will I still affirm Jesus' proclamation that this is the year of the Lord's favor? If I discover there are still the abused, the bullied, the trafficked, and the coerced in our world, will I still affirm Jesus' proclamation that this is the year of the Lord's favor?

Today I declare it, I proclaim it, I confess it. Because of Jesus, I'm in a good year.

11. "Transforming Our World."
12. Hill, "Every One of Us Has a Gift."

Today It Is Fulfilled

Back in the synagogue, Jesus returned the scroll, and took up position to teach. "Today this scripture has been fulfilled in your hearing," he said (Luke 4:21).

Today you can claim a good year in the Lord's favor. You can hear Jesus' proclamation of good news, release, and recovery to the poor, the captives, and the blind. You can claim the poverty, the captivity, and the blindness for yourself, the better to hear Jesus' proclamation of gospel, release, and recovery. You can see the oppressed go free, maybe through death, maybe through miracles in this life, maybe only in faith that sees the invisible and continues to pray in that vision. You can live in the year of the Lord's favor. You can declare and proclaim and confess it with me. Because of Jesus, I'm in a good year.

I'M SURRENDERING, LUKE 4:21-30

Home State Rejection

Salmon P. Chase was born in 1808, in New Hampshire. His father ruled by kindness and died when Salmon was seven years old. At the age of twelve, he went to live with his uncle in Worthington, Ohio. Under his uncle's domineering rule, Salmon learned rigidity, self-denial, and a high evaluation of his own abilities that stayed with him all his life. Upon finishing his education in various states of the union, he returned to Cincinnati determined to be the best lawyer in the city.[13] Chase entered wholeheartedly into politics, helping his state over many hurdles. He was elected to the US Senate for Ohio in 1849,[14] and as the first Republican Governor of Ohio in 1855.[15]

In May 1860, the Republican National Convention met in Chicago. Salmon Chase was among the top three expectant candidates for the nomination for President of the United States. Judge Edward Bates accepted his defeat with composure and went home

---

13. Goodwin, *Team of Rivals*, 34–41.
14. Goodwin, *Team of Rivals*, 134–37.
15. Goodwin, *Team of Rivals*, 181–82.

to be with his family. William Henry Seward took his defeat with brave and gracious dismissal of his fans and celebrants in their profound disappointment. Salmon Portland Chase took the news with bitterness and fury because his Ohio delegation had not supported him unanimously, and he nursed for years the thought that, had they done so, he would have won the presidency.[16]

"'When I remember what New York did for Seward, what Illinois did for Lincoln and what Missouri did for Bates,' Chase told a friend, 'and remember also that neither of these gentlemen ever spent a fourth part—if indeed a tithe of the time labor and means for the Republican Party in their respective states that I have spent for our party in Ohio; and then reflect on the action of the Ohio delegation in Chicago towards me; I confess I have little heart to write or think about it.'"[17]

In his congratulatory letter to Abraham Lincoln, the surprise winner of that coveted nomination, Salmon Chase assumed that the devotion of the Illinois delegation was more gratifying to Lincoln than the nomination itself, citing his rejection by his own Ohio delegation as too much to be borne.[18]

Home state rejection hurts. Any rejection hurts, but hometown rejection is bad. In this chapter, we study the hometown rejection in Nazareth many years ago when Jesus spoke in their synagogue. I think we will learn deeper lessons than merely "do not reject your hometown boys made good." I hope to show you why it is a good thing for me to say "I'm surrendering."

What the Hometown People Said

In the previous chapter, we understood that Luke, the artistic preacher, used this story in his introduction section. After this, Luke used the journey motif to tell the story of Jesus' many interactions and teachings, on the way to his conclusion section showing the outcomes in Jesus' crucifixion and resurrection. Luke used his

16. Goodwin, *Team of Rivals*, 250–251.
17. Goodwin, *Team of Rivals*, 251.
18. Goodwin, *Team of Rivals*, 251.

preacher's art to tell the story to readers who lived centuries ago, and we get to overhear.

The Gospel reading in the previous chapter and this Gospel reading go together as part of the same story. Jesus stopped in various towns in Galilee and began to gather fame. Then he returned to Nazareth, his hometown. In the synagogue on Sabbath, Jesus read from the Isaiah scroll and then prepared to teach from that reading. He appropriated the Isaiah reading to announce his own messiahship, "anointed" meaning Messiah. He said he came to preach good news to the poor, release to the captives, and recovery of sight to the blind. He said he came to let the oppressed go free. He said he proclaimed the year of the Lord's favor. Then he said, "Today this scripture has been fulfilled in your hearing" (Luke 4:1–21). He had preached. He had proclaimed. He had fulfilled this scripture.

He must have said more than this, or maybe the people knew immediately that he was making an astonishing claim and announcement. They said three things.

First, they said, "We know you!" They used the tone that meant, "Come on off your high horse. You're one of us. You're just a kid who used to run around at our feet." It was a rejection of his announcement. There was no honor for him in this town.

Second, the hometown people said, "Do your show here!" It sounded like a dare, like "If you're really the Messiah, prove it here. If you do the things we hear of in other places, do them where we can see them too." The "if" gives them away. It was total doubt. There was no honor for him in this town.

Third, they said, "We don't need you!" Well, you will not find those exact words, yet underlying the other two responses, this one shouts its presence. In proud tones they said, "We're not poor. We're not captive. We're not blind. Neither do we oppress anyone. So, find your do-gooding targets somewhere else."

The dismissive "we know you!" The daring "do your show here!" And the denying "we don't need you!" These are profoundly sad responses to Jesus' proclamation of Messiahship. They shut the Savior out from their hearts and their city. In the end, they escorted him out to throw him over a cliff. Not one voice could be heard saying, "I'm surrendering."

SAVED WITHOUT SWORDS

What Jesus Said

Jesus responded not only to their words but also to their private inner talk. He focused in on their sense of privilege as favored people of God. To break into this, he recalled to their minds two stories from the Hebrew scriptures. The stories come from the only major prophets in the biblical record who did not leave writings for us. Their names mean "My God is Jehovah," and "My God saves." Now the stories.

In the first story, Elijah had hidden safely among the hills for the first part of the famine, then God told him to go live with a widow in Zarephath in Sidon for the remainder of the famine. There were many widows in Israel. Probably many of them knew Elijah. Some of them probably would have been willing to hide and protect him from the king who wanted to kill him. Was he sent to any of them? No, it was a foreigner who lived in a land that honored commerce above God, that God chose as host and that Elijah trusted. God chose for Elijah's ministry a widow not from among the Israelites.

Jesus could see the heated anger building in this room. They were getting the message that Jesus' messiahship was meant to reach the outliers, the marginalized, the hated.

In the second story, Elisha knew of several lepers in Israel. He probably knew where he could find a lot more if he wanted to put on a show of healing someone. Instead, it was Naaman who came for healing, from Syria (Aram) where they worshiped other gods, and Naaman wanted a show. Naaman was offended that the prophet would heal him with no show, not even an appearance. His attendants were finally able to talk him down and they went to the Jordan River to bathe as the prophet had instructed.

Here is one of my little health tips about water. Water is good. Immersion in the bath is good. You do not need mud from the Jordan, but you might use salt, cooked oatmeal, coffee, or herbal tea for various purposes in your bath, besides the wise alternation of hot and cold water. Water is good.

Elisha said Naaman must go to bathe in the Jordan River, and he must do it seven times. Sometimes, when we are trying to stay healthy with the help of water, we give up too soon. Elisha prescribed seven times, and I think he was in his house interceding to God all that time for God to make the mud and herbs work.

Well, Naaman was healed, and he went back to Elisha to pay the prophet. It did not work. There was no commerce and no show in that prophet. This is how Naaman learned not to request a show. He surrendered to the God of heaven and ever after worshiped this God.

The crowd in Nazareth burst into riot at these stories. Many who read this story now think it was because Jesus had put foreigners ahead of Israel by telling these stories in conjunction with his announcement of his Messiahship. I think there was something much deeper toward which Jesus was aiming the power of his word.

No one in that crowd could stomach the idea of surrendering. Instead, they took him out to kill him, and he quietly walked away. No one in that crowd could say, "I'm surrendering."

What the People of Other Towns Said

What did the people of Capernaum and other towns in Galilee say that invited Jesus back? They said three things.

First, they said, "We know you only as you make yourself known." They clung to no preconceived ideas about who Jesus was. They accepted his self-expression. These people of other towns surrendered their tendency to sit in judgment, and simply received the revelation that God saw fit to send.

Second, they said, "We are poor, captive, blind, and oppressed." They were willing to claim position as outliers, marginalized, and hated, in order to hear Jesus' proclamation and be released, recovered, and set free by it. These people of other towns surrendered their tendency to consider themselves more favored by God than others.

Third, they said, "We receive with joy your good news, release, recovery, and freedom." Because they were open to it, they could receive the wonderful proclamations and gifts that Jesus brought for them.

Andrew Murray, who was born in 1828 and who died in 1917, was a South African preacher in the Reformed tradition. He wrote many books for advancement and fulfillment in Christian living.

In one book, entitled, *Humility*, he wrote, "God is faithful. Just as water ever seeks and fills the lowest place, so the moment God finds the creature abased and empty will His glory and power flow in to exalt and to bless."[19]

In another book, entitled *Absolute Surrender*, he wrote, "If I am something, then God is not everything; but when I become nothing, God can become all, and the everlasting God in Christ can reveal Himself fully. That is the higher life. We need to become nothing."[20]

This kind of talk, "abased" and "nothing," sounds scary to some people. No wonder the people in Nazareth rose up against Jesus. On the other hand, there were whole towns where the people could welcome considering themselves nothing, and Jesus could do great things in their towns. They could say, "I'm surrendering."

Surrender

The people of Nazareth gave him the dismissive "we know you!" the daring "do your show here!" and the denying "we don't need you!" Jesus gave them two stories: God sent Elijah to a widow who in a strange land, and God brought to Elisha a man who needed to learn not to request a show. The people of Nazareth had trouble with these stories because they showed God's love going to foreigners, and also because they could not consider themselves like the poor widow or the sick and disgraced man. People in other towns could hear him as he chose to reveal himself, could consider themselves poor, captive, blind, and oppressed, and therefore could receive his proclamations and his release and restoration.

The people in other towns could say "I'm surrendering."

I have discovered I cannot surrender myself. I cannot crucify myself. I cannot beat myself back from that which I crave most.

---

19. Murray, *Humility*, 36–37.
20. Murray, *Absolute Surrender*, 60.

Neither is it done once for all, nor can I be sure it is done for sure. All of that is Jesus' job. My job is to recognize surrender and accept it. This is why I say "I'm surrendering," not "I have surrendered" or "I am surrendered." Neither can I say it for anyone else, either in the negative or the positive, as in "she is surrendered" or "that person is not surrendered." All I can say is, "I'm surrendering." This will keep me from rising up in riot to kill Jesus.

"I'm surrendering."

I'M A SINNER, LUKE 5:1-11

Luke and Simon

Luke was a preacher who told stories. Perhaps he heard this story from someone who was present, or perhaps it was a story circulating which Luke researched and found to be true. He included it in his Gospel which was called by his name, read by many in his time.

Simon, later called Peter by Jesus, and his fellows had fished all night on the Sea of Galilee. They had caught nothing. When they came home in the morning, they found a crowd at the shore, a crowd not only of fishers but also of their families and friends, and many other people from the shoreline villages. The attraction was a man standing on the shore and speaking to the crowd.

Simon had heard that voice before, urgent and restful, forceful and respectful. Simon felt a strong draw to him and a strange hesitance in his presence. Both feelings were new to him, and he had not yet figured them out. He went about his business for some time despite the crowd. Then that voice called out to him. "Simon, could I use your boat? Would you push it out a little way so I can talk to the crowds from it?" The man was already in Simon's boat.

Simon pushed the boat out a little distance and kept doing the important tasks around it. He heard the teaching, the stories, the questions, and the answers. He heard the melody of the voice, the compassionate love in the tones, the common-sense logic of the message.

Then the message got personal. It was a command, directed straight to him and his crew. Jesus said, "Put out [now] into the deep water and let down your nets for a catch" (Luke 5:4).

Nothing could have surprised Simon more. The command was illogical and the commander unqualified in the field of fishing. Simon tried to reason with him, citing how tired and despairing they were, having fished all night and not having caught anything. Of course, the reasoning did not work; the command still stood. Finally, Simon said, "Okay, if you say so, sure we'll do it" (Luke 5:5, author paraphrase).

Luke's telling brings us quickly to the marvelous catch of fish. So large was the haul as to break their nets and sink their boats. To avoid sinking, they called their friends to help, more people to witness the miracle.

Then Simon did the strangest thing. He bowed low before Jesus and cried out in agonized prayer, "Go away from me, Lord, for I am a sinful man!" (Luke 5:8). To parse out exactly what Simon was feeling at that moment would be impossible for us at this distance, but we can guess a few things. Luke's story goes on to say they were amazed and astonished. It might be like I have heard someone say "get out!" when one of their friends gave them a surprising bit of news. Simon did not really mean that he wanted Jesus to leave. In Luke's story, Jesus did not leave and instead chose twelve disciples, Simon, named Peter by his Lord, being one of them.

We might explore right here what Simon meant in saying "I'm a sinner." What might it mean if I were to say "I'm a sinner"? This will necessitate our exploring the meaning of that little big word "sin." The debates over sin have gone on for thousands of years, so we can be sure that we will fall short of touching all parts of the issue. I think this is a good time to remind us that every sermon I preach and every sermon you will ever hear is heresy simply because it can deal with only a part of the whole. It is our goal as preachers to hold some kind of balance or even handling of the topic, but we always fall short. Furthermore, when the topic is God or some such overwhelmingly large dish, then I fall before it as did Simon, blurting out, "I'm a sinner."

First, we will ask "what is sin?" Then we will ask "what does it mean to say 'I'm a sinner'?" Of necessity, what I share will be my own story, my own understandings, colored, I think, by my years with Jesus and the Bible. Perhaps my expressions will encourage you to think again and explore your own understandings.

What Do We Know about Sin?

"What did the preacher talk about?"
"Sin."
"What did the preacher say about sin?"
"He was against it."
This is a folklore story about US President Calvin Coolidge.[21]

I guess we all understand, at the start of this chapter, that sin is the name of something we want to avoid, something we are against. Also, I hope we can all agree primarily that Jesus had none of it, not a smidgen or one tiny bit, not in his DNA, not in his mind, not in his body. Jesus had no sin.

Luke would bear this out for us in showing that Jesus was the one who could forgive sins, and we will extrapolate from this that he was not one of those to be forgiven (Luke 1:77; 5:20–24; 7:37–49; 11:4; 24:47). Jesus had no sin (see also 2 Cor 5:21 and Heb 4:15).

And yet sinners felt safe in, and drawn to, Jesus' presence. Luke shows Jesus often eating and feasting with those whom the good people of society called "sinners" (Luke 5:30; 7:34, 37–49; 15:1–2; 19:7). Actually, I believe Paul when he says all the rest of us have sinned and are sinners (Rom 3:23).

Jesus had no sin. All have sinned. This is a very great difference between Jesus and us. The difference between Jesus and us is enough to make Simon fall on his knees, knowing his smallness and shortfall in this presence of his Lord, and say "I'm a sinner."

What Is Sin?

What then is the definition of sin? Let us work on that.

21. Bapopik@AOL.com, "Coolidge Quote on Preacher and Sin."

Later in his Gospel, Luke tells a story about a man who called Jesus "Good Teacher," as if he, a mere human, could assess and judge what constitutes goodness. Jesus reminded him there is no one good, no one without sin, but God. What the man wanted was a sure trip to goodness, so Jesus played along. "You know the commandments," Jesus said, and then quoted from the Ten Commandments, as if to say "keep these and you will be good, without sin" (1 John 3:4; Rom 13:10; John 14:15; 15:10; 1 John 5:2-3; 1 John 1:6). As the story developed, Jesus had to point out to the man that he had not even kept the first of those ten commandments (Luke 18:18–24).

I am going now straight to the source Jesus cited, the Ten Commandments in Exod 20, but this is not a treatise about the Ten Commandments. Instead, let us simply notice that the very first of the ten bans any other God from our lives except the God who delivered Israel from Egypt, the God of the Bible. The first commandment requires worship, love, and connection to this God. I propose here that the very first sin, and foundational to all other sins, is separation from God. Sin is not primarily all these other things which we say separate us from God; sin *is* separation from God.

Sin is not sex. Some quote Ps 51:5, "in sin my mother conceived me," to say that sin is sex. We will visit some better interpretations in a minute. Sin is not sex. Sin is separation from God.

Sin is not in our bodies. Sin's effects may reside in the body after time, but the body is not the carrier of sin, to be shamed and shunned. The desires of the body for food, sleep, exercise, water, air, and sunlight are put there by God to keep us alive to serve him. Sin is not in our bodies. Sin is separation from God.

According to that definition, I say with conviction, "I'm a sinner."

What Does It Mean to Say, "I'm Born in Sin"?

When we say we were born in sin, we can mean that "separation from God" is the country in which we are born, a country claimed and ruled by the originator of "separation from God." By birth, our citizenship is in a kingdom that is at war with God, "separated from God."

When we say we were conceived in sin, we can mean our heritage was formulated around archetypes and institutions stored in collective memory, which are systems of "separation from God."

When we say we are born in sin, we may be thinking of transgenerational habits and culture whereby neither my parents nor I had any idea what it would be like to have God in our consciousness all the time. Our homing sense, our resting position, our comfort zone always takes us back to "separation from God."

Like Simon, we are hopelessly mired in breaking the first commandment, in "separation from God," in sin. There is a man who can save us, if we can admit "I'm a sinner."

I have no memory of how a total, all-consuming connection with God works. I have no natural caution light for when I have let something else take over the place of God in my life. I lack the habits and culture of continuous connection with God. Instead, I have habits of thought that keep me in the track of "separation from God," the track of sin. I believe this is what Simon felt as he knelt before Jesus. He sensed Jesus' total and continuous connection with God, and that knowledge of Jesus exposed to Simon his own profound dependence on flimsy substitutes. This is the sense in which I can say "I'm a sinner."

What Does It Mean to Say, "I'm a Sinner"?

What does it mean to say, "I'm a sinner"?

"I'm a sinner" is not a shameful statement; it is a courageous, authentic, naked, effective statement of the truth of the matter.

"I'm a sinner" is not an excuse, like an illness, for laziness or inattention; it is a doorway, a tool, a step.

"I'm a sinner" should never be said flippantly, like "What could you expect? I'm a sinner!" Instead, it is a profound and solemn truth that caused the death of the best friend this world ever had.

"I'm a sinner" does not need the word "saved" next to it; Jesus accepts me as a sinner, and so, I hope, do other Christians.

"I'm a sinner" is not giving in to Satan; it is cutting him off at the knees. Whenever he says sneeringly, "You're a sinner!" I say confidently, "Yes, I'm a sinner, and Jesus came to save sinners" (Luke 5:32).

"I'm a sinner" is not blaming God or claiming that God made me junk; I was interfered with in the making. Saying "I'm a sinner" is my claim on God's saving work.

"I'm a sinner" does not lessen my self-esteem or the esteem in which I hold you. I see each of us as perfect for today in God's saving work.

Later Luke showed Jesus telling the story of a good man and a sinner in prayer, the good man parading his goodness and the sinner crying for mercy, admitting, "I'm a sinner." Jesus said the sinner rather than the good man went home made right (Luke 18:9–14).

In the present story, Simon saw himself as a sinner and refused to deny it. I, too, decide anew right now to own my statement, "I'm a sinner."

How I Found Out

I did well as a kid. I grew up in a family that had right and wrong all figured out, and I did the right. No big or little sins for me! In young adulthood I learned that things were not always black and white. I made some mistakes. I sinned. I hurt other people by my sins. I railed at God that he had promised to make me right and he had failed, seeing I had been proven wrong. One wise adult said to me something I will never forget. "Wilma," he said, "you are not nearly as perfect as you think you are. God has a long way to go for most of us." It was a shock to me that I might be more bad than I thought. That was the seed for me, and it grew to be the surest rock in my spiritual logic. "I'm a sinner." I will admit what I see, and that admission is my claim on God's attention. "I'm a sinner" is a badge I will let the world and all good and evil entities in the universe see. "I'm a sinner."

One day, discouraged and depressed, I walked into a recovery group and found it good for me. I read the AA Big Book[22] and thoroughly resonated with it. I wished we had churches where we happily greet one another with something like, "Hello, I'm Wilma, and I'm a sinner."

JERUSALEM WAIL, LUKE 13:31–35

The Fear of God

The little boys were not behaving. They were brothers near in age and seemed intent on driving the community and their mother to distraction. One day she spilled her fears and frustrations to a neighbor friend, who told her, "Oh, that happened to me with my son, too. I just marched him down to the church and made him confess to the priest. That took care of it."

The next day the end-of-her-rope mother took both her boys to see the priest. The first boy went into the small office, looking all around, not sure what to expect. Then the priest spoke: "Young man, where is God?" The little boy ran out, grabbed his brother, and said, "We've got to get out of here! They've lost God and they're trying to pin it on us!"[23]

In this chapter, we will observe the difference between fear and love for motivation. First, we have to find out where we are in Luke. We can notice that we are not in the introduction anymore.

We have followed Jesus from temptations in the wilderness through efforts to minister in his hometown. This was in the introduction. To transition to the body of his Gospel, Luke narrated this famous transition statement: "When the days drew near for him to be taken up, he set his face to go to Jerusalem" (Luke 9:51). It is a statement filled with determination, almost a dread determination.

The central portion of Luke is shaped as a journey. Luke chose the journey form in which to set much of Jesus' ministry, on his way

---

22. "This is the Third Edition of the Big Book, the Basic Text for Alcoholics Anonymous." Anonymous, *Alcoholics Anonymous*, cover.

23. Cook and Baldwin, *Love, Acceptance, and Forgiveness*, 35.

to Jerusalem. You remember Homer's *Odyssey* and Dante's *Divine Comedy* and John Bunyan's *Pilgrim's Progress* are all famous stories telling epic concepts in the journey format. Our reading for this chapter jumps into that journey. We are reading no longer in the introduction to the book. I think we will be picking and choosing a few of Luke's journey stories in the remaining chapters.

The current reading shows two attitudes: one attitude that Jesus could have taken and the other attitude that Jesus did take, on his way to Jerusalem. We have the opportunity to choose fear or love.

Jesus and No Fear

Before we follow our reading and jump right into the middle of the journey, let us observe a little story that happened when Jesus set his face so determinedly to go to Jerusalem. He had been ministering in Galilee which is roughly sixty-five miles from Jerusalem if you could fly. Well, Jesus and his disciples had a worse problem than not being able to fly. The worse problem was that the hated Samaritans occupied the land between Galilee and Jerusalem. To go around would add another thirty miles or so to their trek by foot. Jesus sent word ahead of their coming to the first Samaritan town.

When they came to the town, the townspeople would not receive him because he was headed for Jerusalem. The disciples, James and John, said, "Lord, do you want us to command fire to come down from heaven and consume them?" (Luke 9:51–56). I think they were measuring the insult to their master as worthy of fire from heaven, but Jesus rebuked them instead of the townspeople. Jesus rebuked the two disciples for their punishing spirit, and they walked on. Is fear the thing Jesus wants to engender in people so they will accept him? Maybe not.

In the Gospel reading for this chapter, some religious leaders carried scary rumors to Jesus. They had no protective instinct for Jesus. They wanted him to leave, yet they wanted him to leave from fear rather than from his own choice. Or maybe they wanted to make themselves and the people think that they were the ones who had the power or the savvy to make him leave. Whatever their own motivation, they strongly suggested a motive for Jesus. They said, "You'd better get out of here! Herod wants to kill you!" (Luke 13:31, author paraphrase). You should be afraid and leave.

Well, since Jesus was leaving anyway, this put him in a bind. If he left now after this, the religious leaders would be able to claim they had made him leave, or at the least had shown the people that Jesus was a coward. Jesus cleared up the matter.

"You go and tell that fox," he said, clearly laying the responsibility back on their shoulders. "I continue freeing and curing people until I'm ready to go. And when I go, it will be because no prophet should be killed outside of Jerusalem" (Luke 13:31–33, author paraphrase). It will not be because you want me to go or because of some fear you want me to carry.

For Jesus? No fear! I propose that it is important for us to consider our motives. If someone has put fear in us, it is important to face the fear and reclaim our decisions so they can be made without fear. I do not do this well. I often wish I had the quick words that Jesus seemed to have (but oh well, I would probably be a bumbling Peter if I had quick words). If I operate out of fear, I am the more likely to act in punishing ways to put the fear of God in others. Or if others perceive me to be acting out of fear, they will believe that they, too, can use fear, and pile on the fear.

For Jesus? No fear! Yet he went to Jerusalem. He did not interrupt or stop his determination either from fear or from others' perception that he might be fearful. He went on to Jerusalem.

Jesus Saves

Before going on to complete our comparison of fear and love as motivations in Jesus' life, let us stop and consider some other passages in Luke that will illumine who Jesus is and why he came. As Jesus and his disciples were turning away from the town mentioned earlier which some of the disciples thought needed to burn, Jesus said, "The Son of Man has not come to destroy the lives of human beings but to save them" (Luke 9:56, footnote). Jesus saves!

Saved without Swords

It is not merely that Jesus brings us love as a better motivation, but also the Bible teaches that Jesus saves from a life of fear and unlove. There is something more drastic that I need than a little more love, I need to be saved from enemies and myself who have enrolled and enlisted me in the ways of greed, fear, shame, and guilt. It is that enrollment from which I must be rescued and saved. Jesus saves!

You remember Mary's reaction when she heard it confirmed by her cousin Elizabeth that she was to be the mother of the Messiah. She burst out singing, "My soul magnifies the Lord, and my spirit rejoices in God my Savior" (Luke 1:47). She went on to mention Abraham and his descendants as the holders of the promise which God is remembering by sending this Savior. Mary believed Jesus saves.

You also remember Zechariah's reaction. This is cousin Elizabeth's husband speaking during the naming of their son, John, who would become the announcer of Jesus. Zechariah said of God, "He has raised up a mighty savior . . . as he spoke through the mouth of his holy prophets from old, that we would be saved" (Luke 1:69–71). Zechariah went on to mention Abraham as the ancestor and holder of the holy covenant that calls for this saving event. Jesus would be the savior. Zechariah believed Jesus saves.

Let us now turn to a question which Luke placed immediately prior to the comments about fear in our reading for this time. Someone asked Jesus, "Lord, will only a few be saved?" (Luke 13:23). Jesus answered with parables about the narrow door and the shut door with apparently the God figure in the parable having the power to open the door if he knows the knockers. The question, "Who can be saved?" was on the minds of the common people.

The same question, Who can be saved? will be on our minds as we finish our work in Luke and turn to Romans later in this book. One thing I believe we can nail down right now is that Jesus saves! I am forever grateful.

Jesus and Love

Luke's story does not let Jesus move on from that encounter with some religious leaders without showing his love. Jesus turned the tricky interaction into an impassioned lament. "Jerusalem, Jerusalem, the city that kills the prophets and stones those who are sent to it! How often have I desired to gather your children together as a hen gathers her brood under her wings, and you were not willing!" (Luke 13:34).

This is one of the few instances in the Bible of describing God or Jesus by use of a feminine metaphor. To balance it, I will show you a masculine metaphor from Jer 31:10. "He who scattered Israel will gather him, and will keep him as a shepherd a flock." Therefore, whether you can see Jesus better as a hen or as a shepherd, the point is still the same. Jesus loved Jerusalem!

Jerusalem had killed prophets and others sent to it. Jerusalem had renounced and ridiculed the offer of Jesus' love. Yet Jesus still loved Jerusalem! Despite all the insulting rejection, Jesus still wanted to gather them up into his love. He wanted to bring them close to him. He wanted them to feel respected and free in his care. Jesus' love knew no limit and no exception. Jesus loved Jerusalem.

The thought comes to me that someone might worry that Jesus loved a city, a system, a nation, and not any individuals for themselves. This is a political concern that has been part of discussions and wars throughout the ages.

The political journalist Howard Fineman writes about "the thirteen American arguments," at least four of which circle around the issue of the individual versus the government, around the balances between personal, individual, local, national, and presidential power.[24]

From reading Fineman's work, I come away to ask questions that are on the minds of many. What are the responsibilities and freedoms of individuals versus those of the government? What are the responsibilities and freedoms of states versus those of the federal office? What are the responsibilities and freedoms of nations versus those of global governance? What are the duties and benefits

---

24. Fineman, *Thirteen American Arguments*, 21–37, 92–107, 141–177.

of church members versus the duties and benefits of the church? It is part of an ongoing conversation. Every time you attend church, this will be some of your consideration. Does Jesus love me for myself? Or only through a church? Or is it some mix of both? And what will I give to and receive from my church?

I believe Jesus loves you! I believe Jesus loves our churches! Both! I cannot say just what mixture of individual or community duties you will find most in agreement with God's call on your life. God will let you know. I hope you choose to attend church and listen to God.

There are very many stories of our Lord spending specific love and energy on one person, individually. Further, there are many parables, the stories Jesus told, that highlight the beloved value of one individual. There are enough of these so that we need a few of the instances like that in our reading for this chapter, to recognize that Jesus also loves churches. He gave himself for the church (Eph 5:25). He sent to churches specialized letters expressing his care (Rev 1–3).

Jesus loved Jerusalem. Jesus' love for Jerusalem was loyal, long lasting, and long suffering. Jesus' love for Jerusalem allowed no room for fear, in him, in any individual, or in the church. He mourned, "Jerusalem, Jerusalem!"

Love, Acceptance, and Forgiveness

Jesus refused the fear, shame, and guilt that others wanted him to feel. Instead, he maintained always his own love, acceptance, and forgiveness.[25] Jesus' love respects you. Jesus' love releases you. Jesus' love gathers you to himself. Let the Holy Spirit bring to you the sense of Jesus' protective and comforting wings closing down around you to give you what you have always wanted and needed.

Jerry Cook and Stanley Baldwin wrote a book several years ago that helped to shape my thinking about love, acceptance, and

---

25. From the provocative and thorough title of Cook and Baldwin's book, *Love, Acceptance, and Forgiveness.*

forgiveness in church. This quotation from him describes for me Jesus' love for you and me and our church.

"The minimal guarantee we must make to people is that they will be loved—always, under every circumstance, with no exception. The second guarantee is that they will be totally accepted, without reservation. The third thing we must guarantee people is that no matter how miserably they fail or how blatantly they sin, unreserved forgiveness is theirs for the asking with no bitter taste left in anybody's mouth."[26]

With this kind of love, or at least with the sincere effort to give this kind of love, Pastor Cook's church grew from 23 to more than 4,500 in 14 years. Talk about church growth! Yes.

Jesus loved Jerusalem. He cried, "Jerusalem, Jerusalem!" despite all their insults of his love. Jesus loves our church, your church. Jesus loves you.

Let us not make him cry in the same sadness over us, "Jerusalem, Jerusalem."

WHAT DAD WANTED, LUKE 15:1-3, 11-32

A Story of Three People

Does anyone here know a family of parents with exactly two sons, only two boys and no girls? If you do know of such a set of brothers, then you may be ahead of the story we will discuss in this chapter. Two brothers seem to be a theme in the origin stories recorded in the Torah. There are Cain and Abel, Ishmael and Isaac, Esau and Jacob, and Manasseh and Ephraim. Jesus told several stories about two sons and this, in Luke 15, is the only one recorded by Luke.

The parable of the generous father and two wasteful sons was told by Jesus along his journey to Jerusalem. The prompt for the story was the complaint by the religious leaders and scribes that Jesus ate with sinners. Now follow the logic with me for a moment. Seems like this fact yields the observation that there were two groups in front of Jesus, the sinners and the non-sinners. Maybe

---

26. Cook and Baldwin. *Love, Acceptance, and Forgiveness*, 11.

there were some others present, but those are the groups brought into view in this conversation.

I will re-tell the story, including a few insights about how people who live in the Middle East would have understood the parable. Many of these insights come from a book by Kenneth E. Bailey,[27] who lived and taught for forty years in Cyprus, Jerusalem, Lebanon, and Egypt.

I will re-tell the story, looking especially for what each of the boys wanted, in preparation for dwelling a bit on what dad wanted.

What the Two Boys Wanted

The younger son wanted cash, money, and later, food. First, he wanted his father dead so he could have the inheritance, sell it, and walk away rich. The estate was large, large enough to have plenty of fattened calves, and a ballroom big enough to seat a crowd large enough to finish off a fattened calf in one evening. There were servants and slaves and hired musicians.

The father would be expected to slap the audacious son and kick him out of the house. Instead, he gave him half the estate, and he gave him the right to sell. The words "gathered all he had" connote selling, turning it all into cash. And who would buy? Why, the community would buy! The people who lived across the narrow street, so narrow they could put a plank across between windows and carry bread across so as not to break the Sabbath. The shame and humiliation of this family was in imminent danger of evoking the "cutting off" ceremony by which the community would together begin the shaming and shunning of an unworthy son.

The younger son completed his sales in haste and set out to put distance quickly between him and the home village. Far away he lived wastefully, luxuriously, and indolently; in short, prodigally. Whore expenses were not mentioned. When the money was gone, the young man tried to find a job, but no one would pay him anything. Only then did he start realizing the enormity of his debt. If ever he was to go back home, he must arrive with gifts besides all

---

27. Bailey, *Jacob and the Prodigal*, 95–117.

the money, but if no one would give him a job or a salary, how could he get the money? How could he get food?

This is not the repentance part of the story. The Bible says he came to himself, not that he came to God or came to Jesus. He did some hard reckoning on himself and returned to his own manipulative ways. Notice that his plan said nothing about becoming one of his father's slaves. No, what he wanted was an endorsement in order to get an apprenticeship so he could work to pay off the debt. There was no repentance of his manipulations or his belief in money as the best good. No, like all the other lost items in Luke 15, the younger son was incapable of coming back on his own; he must be rescued. He must be saved.

The father had his own plan to rescue this lost boy. The plan was to watch, always watch, so as to see the returning son before anyone else in the village could recognize him and set the shame-bomb on him. This took time from the father's other endeavors. As soon as he saw his son a long way off, he picked up his long robes and ran. He ran bare-legged and all. What a strange and shameful sight to see a well-respected rich man streaking through town. This was enough to gather stares, and that is how it came about that the whole village saw the father embrace and repeatedly kiss this returning son. They saw servants running out beyond the town with rich clothing and shoes. They saw the father reclothe his son and then walk him through their crowds inviting all along the way to come to a celebration feast at his house. Yes, he would eat with this sinner, and he wanted them to do so, also. Thus, the father figure became Jesus, the one who eats with sinners.

Did you notice the celebration is because of the father's reception of his son back from death, not because of the prodigal's return? The boy is not the hero of the story; the father is the hero in his watch and rescue against the shame on his boy. Jesus is the hero of our stories.

The older son did not distinguish the correct hero. He asked one of the slaves, and was told the reason for the celebration, that the father had received his son safe and sound. He thought they were celebrating his brother without even asking him to pay anything for his sins. He went on the attack, accusing the father of stinginess with him, the stable brother, and accusing the younger brother of consorting with harlots. Using a harlot called for stoning in old Hebrew texts, much more shameful and deadly than a mere cutting off ceremony. The older brother wanted his younger brother to pay for being a sinner.

The father also had a plan for rescuing this older son, the "non-sinner." He got up from among his feast guests, gathered up his long robes, and ran out barelegged to meet his son coming in from the field. He rescued his older son from saying shameful things in front of the community at feast. He heard the boy's accusations himself without reaction, and repeated the reason for the feast: "this brother of yours was dead and has come to life; he was lost and has been found" (Luke 15:32). More importantly, besides saving the family from more shame, the father rescued his younger son from having to express and entrench attitudes of fear, shame, and guilt. This was the same effort he was putting out for his older son, to keep him from having to express and entrench attitudes of fear, shame, and guilt.

It is not the return that is celebrated; it is the finding. It is the fact that the younger son accepts to be found. The sinner accepts the finding. Will the non-sinner accept the finding? If he does, he must accept his younger brother, the sinner, as a person similarly found. He must accept the compassion of the father for himself as well as for the sinner brother. The story remains unfinished, with the older brother wanting the younger brother to pay, yet that fact in no way diminishes the shining portrayal of the father's love as costly in money, in time, and in humiliation.

What Dad Wanted

What did Dad want? The younger son wanted cash and then food. The older son wanted the younger son to pay. What did Dad want? I will give you my observations, informed by reading Edwin Friedman's work as author and lecturer on leadership, family, and other emotional processes.[28] I will start from the pieces of evidence we

---

28. Friedman, *Failure of Nerve*, 29–228.

have in the story, that here there are several systems intertwining, and inter-reacting with anxiety and resulting fear, shame, and guilt. Here are seven things that Dad wanted.

The father wanted play! Yes, play! In a system where the only solution others think of is to try harder, work harder, and manipulate smarter, Jesus says, "We ought to make merry!"

The father wanted differentiation. In a system where everyone knew how things ought to be done, and everyone went along to get along, Jesus says, "For something you care about, go ahead and be different!"

The father wanted decision. In a system where information is everything, where what one did out in the far country needs to be dug up and haggled over, Jesus says, "Everything is yours; just decide to come in."

The father wanted adventure. In a system where everyone wants a sure deal with certainty, whether by cunning manipulation of the system or by impeccable work ethic, Jesus says, "I want to see him in the best robe, the family ring, and good shoes. It is my adventure to watch what he does with them."

The father wanted choice. In a system where someone's reaction determines whole courses of action, rather than pondering alternatives bathed in love, acceptance, and forgiveness, and in this way letting true choices emerge, Jesus says, "You can choose not to label people sinners or non-sinners. You can choose to withhold your reaction until you have actually experienced the party."

The father wanted to support the various strengths of his sons. In a system where people become pigeonholed by the time they enter school and blamed for innumerable faults, Jesus said, "Give him a fattened calf so he's not hungry or in need anymore, and let's see what his art will do."

The father wanted to support the process and the time that process takes. In a system where people readily take on extreme and shared anxiety to quick-fix our problems now, Jesus says, "Come in, taste, dance, do not be afraid, for I am with you."

What Dad wanted was more than just peace between the brothers. What Dad wanted was more than just a party where everyone enjoys him or herself. What Dad wanted was to find his sons in situations where they could accept being found without all their baggage of trying harder, going along to get along, demanding information, craving certainty, reacting to reactions, blaming, and rushing to fix.

What Dad wanted was to rescue his sons from the systems of anxiety in which they were intertwined and entangled so they could actually spend some time with him.

Compare to Isaac, Jacob, and Esau

Kenneth Bailey proposes that in telling the parable of the father and two sons, Jesus re-told and reshaped the story of Israel.[29] In telling his story, Jesus made the father strong, a fit metaphor for God, as Isaac was not. He made the exile about inheritance and money as was Jacob's story. He made the younger son have to hurry to get out of town, as did Jacob, and go attach himself to a citizen of the new land for work in animal husbandry, like Jacob. If we agree with Bailey's understanding, both the younger brother and Jacob made manipulative speeches on returning home. Jacob had made money and gifts in the far country, while the younger son came home empty-handed. Both Esau, Jacob's older brother, and the older son worked in the field, came in from the field to find that injustice was occurring, and became very angry. Both fathers tried to reason with their older sons.

Jesus rewrote the story of Jacob in making the father strong and then compassionate and willing to make costly sacrifices, a fit representation of himself. Jesus rewrote the story in making the ending an unfinished cliff-hanger, so we do not know whether the older son was rescued.

How will our story finish? Do you know what Dad wants in your case? Will you accept being found and come in to the banquet? Will you sit beside fellow found people with compassion?

Will you spend time with Jesus? That is what Dad wanted.

---

29. Bailey, *Jacob and the Prodigal*, 136–94.

HIDDEN SAYINGS, LUKE 18:28-34

Hidden from Them

When was the last time your pair of glasses or your phone was hiding from you? In school, was there a class you took for which the material seemed to be hiding from you, so you could not grasp or remember it? Are there parts of the Bible that seem hidden? Does truth seem hidden today?

There is one set of sayings by Jesus that Luke describes as hidden. I find those sayings fascinating and I want to explore them with you now. You remember Luke wrote his Gospel in the form of a travel story, a journey into which to fit all the items he wanted to say about Jesus. Luke made a proper introduction before starting the journey story and then a clear transition in Jesus' setting his face to go to Jerusalem.

Luke may have written during the time of Nero, the fifth of the first eight Roman Caesars after the senate voted Julius Caesar in as a god upon his death on March 15, in 44 BCE. By this time, the Roman infrastructure of roads and aqueducts was thorough, complex, and efficient. To think about taking a journey was much easier now than, say, when Homer wrote *The Odyssey* five hundred years earlier. One major problem for Christianity and for Luke as its chronicler was the fact that all the Caesars considered themselves sons of god and anyone claiming to be the son of God would be considered a rebel, to be killed in order to keep the peace. Luke, writing primarily to non-Jews in the Roman Empire, never used the name Son of God for Jesus, perhaps in an effort not to prejudice people too soon. He used the name Son of David instead, knowing that folk familiar with the Hebrew Scriptures would recognize this as reference to the Messiah.

Luke told Jesus' story as a journey from Galilee to Jerusalem. The sayings we will examine now, those that were hidden, have one set just before Jesus set his face to go to Jerusalem and another set just before Jesus entered Jerusalem on the first Palm Sunday. The first set of these sayings helps close out the introduction; the second set helps close out the journey, to enter into the conclusion, which we usually think about at Easter time.

What would be hidden from the disciples or the people of Israel? What things seem hidden to us today? Is there a reason? Let us explore the hidden sayings of Jesus.

Who Is the Greatest? Luke 9:22–23, 44–45

Suddenly Peter knew who Jesus was. It was a light bulb moment, a solution of all puzzles and release from all dead ends. Jesus was the Messiah of God! Jesus had asked who the crowds say he is, and then who the disciples say he is. He took a poll, and in the middle of the poll, everything suddenly came together for Peter, and he said bluntly, "The Messiah of God!" (Luke 9:18).

Please do not get worried about Luke's quote from Peter being different from Matthew's. Newspapers today would not agree, except they all quote each other or the one authorized version. This is Luke's version of Peter's "aha!" moment.

Jesus said in a surprisingly stern voice, "Please don't tell anyone" (Luke 9:21, author paraphrase).

Then he said, "The Son of Man [referring to himself] must undergo great suffering, and be rejected by the elders, chief priests, and scribes, and be killed, and on the third day be raised" (Luke 9:22). Don't get caught up in the glory of the revelation, because there are two sides to this wonder. Further, Jesus said anyone who wants to be his disciple must deny self and take up the cross daily and follow him, Jesus.

What a strange and cryptic saying that must have been! They knew about crosses. And they knew about carrying the cross. Many times, the condemned person was made to carry to the execution site the piece of wood on which he would impaled, sometimes already affixed to it. Carrying the cross was a horrible thing. It announced a shameful death and attracted compulsive stares. It showcased the power of one person over another and the powerlessness of the human condition in the face of bullying and tyranny.

Surely Jesus could not have meant that, yet they did not ask him what he meant.

Eight days later they had a fabulous revelation experience on the mountain as they saw their Lord in shining, dazzling brightness and wondered what to do about it. Then the Lord healed a most intense and stubborn case, and all the people stood still in awe, ready to tell about it once they got their words back.

While they were in that state of amazement, Jesus said, "Let these words sink into your ears: The Son of Man is going to be betrayed into human hands" (Luke 9:44). They did not understand it. It was hidden, concealed from them. They could not penetrate the enigma. And they were afraid to ask him. Instead, they started up their argument about who among them was the greatest. This dark saying about the blackest of futures could not be comprehended by them. Its meaning was hidden from them. Why? Because they really wanted to debate and prove who of them was the best. I do not know, was it about being the greatest singer of psalms, the greatest in physical strength, the greatest in ability to coerce others, the greatest preacher, the greatest healer, the greatest money handler? They expected to be placed in high places in the new kingdom of the Messiah. And the saying was hidden from them. This was one of the hidden sayings of Jesus before he even started on his journey to Jerusalem.

With Humility, Luke 18:31–34

The second hidden saying comes after two specific parables and a follower instance, and their order of presentation is instructive. First, the parable of the unjust judge was told to teach the need to pray and keep praying. Second, the parable of two people praying in the temple was given to teach the need to pray and keep on praying, with humility. Third, the instance of the would-be follower, who was rich both in keeping the law and in possessions and could not give them up, was effectively positioned to bring forth the question "then who can be saved?" There is that question again. It was always close to the surface. Jesus said, "What is impossible for mortals is possible for God" (Luke 18:26–27). Pretty much, you cannot save yourself.

Peter mistook the whole cycle and said, "We've left so much to follow you; what do we get?" (Luke 18:29, author paraphrase). Jesus settled Peter with a promise and then said, "See, we are going up to Jerusalem, and everything that is written about the Son of Man by the prophets will be accomplished. For he will be handed over to the Gentiles; and he will be mocked and insulted and spat upon. After they have flogged him, they will kill him, and on the third day he will rise again" (Luke 18:31–33). The saying was hidden from them. They could not understand or grasp it at all.

You can see that the hidden sayings have to do with Jesus' death and his own soon-coming humiliation. Luke, as an artistic preacher, placed these sayings so as to capture the reader's attention while leaving the disciples in the dark. This is the best in literary irony.

Furthermore, Luke showed Jesus hinting that someone else understands. In close conjunction with the record of both these sayings are little snippets about the children, the infants, coming to Jesus (Luke 9:47–48; 18:15–17). They were being affirmed by Jesus as understanding the humility required, thus having greater humility than the disciples had. More delicious irony.

In Luke 10:21, between the record of these two sayings about the cross, Luke recorded Jesus as having gratitude in prayer to God that the Father had "hidden these things from the wise and the intelligent and [had] revealed them to infants." In the context of this prayer, it is clear that the infants were the unschooled disciples who had recently returned from a missionary excursion in which they had great success, and the wise and intelligent to whom the work of God was hidden were the religious leaders of the day with their doctorates and debates and detours from God. Here the disciples were the celebrated ones who understood the things hidden from others. Yet in the big picture, they could not understand the sayings about the cross. They were the hidden sayings.

If Only You Had Recognized, Luke 19:42

A few more days after Jesus' latest attempt to warn his disciples of his looming shaming and death, Jesus arranged his entrance into Jerusalem. No white steed for him, no marching boots, no victory trumpets. He rode a donkey. Barefoot children accompanied him. They carried foliage, branches and fronds from trees to wave in their joy and his honor. He paused the procession as he looked down over the city. He wept with great sobs and said, "If you, even you, had only recognized on this day the things that make for peace! But now they are hidden from your eyes" (Luke 19:42). Jesus saw the future, those who would shortly shame him being shamed and broken with their city lying in ruins, their successes up in flames, their wealth stolen. If only you had given in to me. If only you had stopped your striving for success and for the greatest places among yourselves. If only you had been able to hear that the cross and the third day rising are part of the same saying, the same weekend, the same world-saving event. If only you could have heard the hidden sayings.

You cannot have the success without the surrender. You cannot have the resurrection without the cross. You cannot have freedom from bickering and the rat race without giving up to Jesus. You cannot make your relationships work without coming to the end of scrambling to fill your own needs. You cannot stay sober and in recovery, whether from alcohol or from sin, without admitting that you are powerless to control your life or the lives of others. You cannot build a non-anxious church where miracles happen and people attend out of amazement without giving up the manipulative "go along to get along" mentality, the never-ending cycle of reaction to reaction to reaction.

These are the hidden sayings of Jesus, hidden from his disciples, hidden from Jerusalem in his day, hidden from us. Oh, I hope they are not hidden from us.

SAVED WITHOUT SWORDS

Remember His Words, Luke 24:6-8

The horrible day came and went. Jesus was dead. All their hopes were vanished. There was no kingdom in which to be greatest. There was no procession of joy to lead. There was no Jesus to whom to come as little children in their grief, though the women came to Jesus anyway, in the tomb.

The leaders of the people had scoffed, and the words twisted the people's insides. "He saved others; let him save himself if he is the Messiah of God, his chosen one!" (Luke 23:35). He had not saved himself, and no one flagged the "if" for the people to get wise. Two people, intent on getting out of town, hooked up with a stranger and wailed, "But we had hoped that he was the one to redeem [save] Israel" (Luke 24:21).

At this point, they were all close to coming finally to understand the hidden sayings. What they saw in the tomb instead of Jesus were two men in dazzling white clothes who said to them, "Remember how he told you, while he was still in Galilee, that the Son of Man must be handed over to sinners, and be crucified, and on the third day rise again" (Luke 24:6-7) And they remembered. They finally heard. They finally knew that Jesus saves because he did not save himself. They would remember the hidden sayings.

3

Romans

Who Can Be Saved, and How?

NOT ASHAMED, ROM 1:16-17

The Jews wanted signs for proof. The Greeks wanted ideas to be analyzed. The gospel must be experienced before you know it is true. Yet, to the Jews the gospel seemed wrong, and to the Greeks it seemed foolishness. Despite all this, Paul was "not ashamed of the gospel; it is the power of God for salvation to everyone who has faith" (Rom 1:16).

I lived in a bubble of shame. "You ought to be ashamed of yourself," I was told—and I already was! I tried to dilute the shame I felt. I smiled a lot. I played the organ for church and the piano for the children's department, and I cleaned the church, and I mowed its lawn. I went out on every mission trek conceivable. I carried a large purse stuffed with everything anyone else might possibly want or need in an emergency, so as to be always helpful and kind—and to dilute the shame. I am sure I passed the shame on to others as my elders did to me.

I was shamed over my looks, over my voice, over my grades, and over my friends. I worked hard on those items, trying to wash the shame away. Shame sticks. Shame has a smell that remained in my nose and contaminated everything. Shame has mind pictures that woke me at night with a start. I hung my head and hid around corners. I worked all day and all night. I tried to dilute the shame I felt.

Paul was not ashamed. The gospel of Christ is the power of God for salvation to everyone who believes.

Some people think of the ashes used in worship at the beginning of Lent as a sign of human shame. I will not go there. Jesus has set me free from shame, and I am not going back! Some people think my emphasis on confession and surrender is admission of shame. I refuse that connotation. Confession and surrender to God are not shameful stances. Admitting my addictions and hubris is not shameful. Even if I confess every day and stand continually in the stance of admitting and surrender to God, this is not shame! This is the only means of removing shame!

It is this gospel of Christ that is the power of God for salvation to everyone who believes.

Paul said we get to rejoice in the hope of the glory of God, and hope does not make a person ashamed (Rom 5:2, 5). By God's grace I have hope that lets me fall on my face in confession and surrender with no shame at all.

Jesus even went all the way to the cross in surrender to God, all the while rejecting and refusing the shame that humans wanted to heap on him (Heb 12:2).

Paul quoted the Old Testament prophet Isaiah twice to assure us that whoever believes on Jesus will not be ashamed (Isa 28:16; Rom 9:33; 10:11). There is no shame to the person who believes on Jesus.

Though I bow in confession every day, though repentance courses through me like an avalanche at times, though I admit my limitation and offenses, I have no shame. "I am not ashamed of the gospel; it is the power of God for salvation to everyone who has faith" (Rom 1:16).

In this last chapter of this book, we will walk soberly through Romans. We will tackle Paul's logic to ask the question, Who can be saved, and how? This, then, is that to which the first two thirds of this book have been leading. If you need to catch a break from the logic, feel free to go back and review some of the stories.

In C. S. Lewis's last novel, set in pre-Christian times in a country lying on the edges of civilization, he wrote about two sisters. One sister, the younger and more beautiful one, experienced seeing the god. She tried to describe for her sister what she felt.

> "When I saw [the god], I was neither glad nor afraid (at first). I felt ashamed," she said.
> "But what of? Psyche, they hadn't stripped you naked or anything!"
> "No, no, Maia. Ashamed of looking like a mortal—ashamed of being a mortal."
> "But how could you help that?"
> "Don't you think the things people are most ashamed of are the things they can't help?"[1]

Later:

> "Oh, Maia, you still don't understand. This shame has nothing to do with He or She. It's the being mortal—being, how shall I say it? . . . insufficient. Don't you think a dream would feel shy if it were seen walking about in the waking world?"[2]

Still later, after a good deal more thinking the older sister affirmed, "We are king's daughters, still."[3]

We are insufficient, but king's daughters and sons. We are confessing, admitting, repenting, but not ashamed, because of the gospel of Christ.

---

1. Lewis, *Till We Have Faces*, 111.
2. Lewis, *Till We Have Faces*, 114–15.
3. Lewis, *Till We Have Faces*, 138.

SAVED WITHOUT SWORDS

MOSES AND ME, ROMANS 3:19-24, 27-28, 31

The Story of Rome

They were twins, sons of Mars, the god, set adrift in a basket on the Tiber River. The little basket finally came to rest on shore at the future site of the city of Rome. There a mother wolf befriended them and let them suck her milk. Then a shepherd found them and raised them. As adults they founded a city. Romulus built a wall, Remus jumped over it, and Romulus killed him. From then on, the city was called Rome.[4]

There is evidence of settlements around Rome as far back as 1000 BCE. The myth of Romulus and Remus is dated 753 BCE. Rome defeated Macedon and took over the Greek empire in 168 BCE. This opened all of the fertile crescent to Roman rule; therefore, the tiny kingdom of the Jews became one of Rome's outlying holdings. Then in 146 BCE, Rome defeated her last remaining competition, the African city of Carthage, and became the uncontested empire of the world.[5]

By the time Paul wrote his letter to the Romans, the hand of the Roman Empire was felt all over the western world, although the language was Greek. Rome both conquered and submitted to the Greek culture. If you were there you could be a Roman citizen and a Greek philosopher at the same time. Greek culture was called Hellenism after the ancient name for Greece, Hellas. The people to whom Paul wrote the letter were living in Rome. By the time Paul wrote, they were probably all Greeks, too, by language and culture, except that Paul did know of some whom he called barbarians (Rom 1:14). They would be those without the Greek culture.[6]

We have reviewed who the Romans were and who the Greeks were. Next, we need to explore who the Jews were because, in his letter to the Romans, Paul sometimes speaks of the Jews and the Greeks in the same breath while showing their differences. (Some

---

4. Editors of Encyclopaedia Britannica, "Romulus and Remus."
5. History.com Editors, "Ancient Rome."
6. Scott, *Real Paul*, 56.

translations use the word "gentiles" here rather than Greeks, Rom 1:16; 3:9, 29; 9:24.)

The Story of Moses

Long before the myth of Romulus and Remus had even been conceived, there was Adam. Some people call him a myth, too. I do not. Adam came fresh off the creative hand of God, with the purposes of eternity inscribed in every fiber and cell. Adam was meant to live forever. Actually, there were two of them, perfectly complementary in their fit to keep always maturing. Distressingly, Adam and Eve chose to believe a liar rather than God and the liar got to run the world.

The situation got so bad under the new rulership that God called a halt. He used Noah to save a few and start over. And things got so bad again that God pulled Abraham out of the mix, saying God would make Abraham's family a blessing to all families of the earth. Abraham's family needed a place to incubate and populate, for which reason God sent them to Egypt for four hundred years. Then he raised up Moses to lead them back home. Moses is the one through whom God gave the law, the Ten Commandments, and other statutes and precepts. Scholars debate whether it was two or four centuries later that David was established on the throne of Israel—still Abraham's family, Abraham's descendants, being a blessing to all families of the earth. David reigned about 1000 BCE, the same time the peninsula of Rome was first being settled.

Nevertheless, David's descendants did not do so well at following God. The whole northern section of Israel got raided and subjugated, the people dispersed in other lands. In Judah, as the southern part of Israel was called, one day around 600 BCE, Josiah the king was surprised to be told there was a law, a book that had been found in a temple clean-up campaign. Josiah tried to clean up their actions according to that law, but it was too late. Soon, God let Judah go into captivity to a nation who worshiped other gods. There they began to be called Jews, short for Judah. The word "gentile" came into biblical use at about the same time as did the word

"Jews." "Gentile" may mean someone who is not Israelite, someone who is not Jewish, or even, in Paul, perhaps someone who is not Christian.

Now we have reviewed who the Jews were, and in the process, we have touched on Moses, the law, and gentiles. We are ready to examine Paul's letters and some of the ways he used these words in his letter to the Romans. Let us remember, Paul was writing to Romans, most of whom were steeped in the Greek culture called Hellenism. He used the word "gentiles" (and Greeks in some translations) most of the time for those who were simply not Jews (Rom 1:16; 3:9, 29; 9:24).

The Story of Paul's Epistles

One of Paul's tricks in the letter to the Romans that I find most challenging and fun is his use of the word "law." In fact, I suggest that whenever we come across that word "law" in Romans maybe we would do well to stop and ponder just what law is meant by the word in that case. I think Paul enjoyed puns. There is the law of Moses called the Torah. There is the law of the Ten Commandments. There is the law that talks about personal sanitation, food choices, and feast days. These all could be called the law of Moses. Then there are Paul's additions. There is the law of sin that drags you down like the law of gravity. There is the law of the Spirit of Christ which determines that he will not fail to bring life. Then there are also other laws to describe the way things just seem to be without further reason. Paul's first readers would have been much quicker than we are to understand the punchlines.

However, Paul's letter to the Romans is full of much more than just religious punchlines. The letter we call Romans is like no other. To the Thessalonians, Corinthians, and Galatians, Paul wrote in red-hot, raw-video mode, dealing specifically with urgent, current issues in the respective churches. One might even say that Corinthians and especially Galatians are in some ways precursors to Romans. By the time Paul wrote Romans, he had had time to organize his thoughts. Some find in Romans the most logical argument for believing in Christ of those presented anywhere in the Bible.

In fact, perhaps a quick summary here will show us some of the clarity of logic and organization in the Epistle to the Romans. Here's my outline by chapters: (1) Gentiles Are Sinners, (2) Jews Are Sinners, (3) All Are Sinners, (4) Lessons from Abraham, (5) Lessons from Adam, (6) Dead with Jesus, (7) Staying Dead with Jesus, (8) Living Anew with Jesus, (9–12) Jews and Gentiles. Perhaps it is easy now to see how our work will progress through Moses to Abraham, then to Adam, to new life in Christ, and finally to a consideration of Paul's work with Jews and gentiles.

Perhaps you can see from this very long introduction that the main questions in the Epistle to the Romans are first, Who can be saved? Can Greeks or gentiles really be saved? And second, How does salvation happen? In this chapter, we will quickly examine the first three chapters of Romans where Moses and the law are cited, to see if we can find answers to these two questions.

Who Can Be Saved?

We have cited these statements earlier. Now let us examine them.

Rom 1:16: "For I am not ashamed of the gospel; it is the power of God for salvation to everyone who has faith, to the Jew first and also to the Greek." Jews and Greeks can be saved.

Rom 3:9: "What then? Are we any better off? No, not at all; for we have already charged that all, both Jews and Greeks, are under the power of sin." Jews are not better than Greeks and gentiles.

Rom 3:23: "For there is no distinction, since all have sinned and fall short of the glory of God." Jews and gentiles are all sinners.

Rom 3:29: "Or is God the God of Jews only? Is he not the God of Gentiles also? Yes, of Gentiles also." Gentiles, those who are not Jews, can be saved.

Who can be saved? Everyone. Everyone who buys into the fact that we all have sinned and need to be saved. Of course, the person who knows no need of salvation will not even be asking these questions. The answer to the first question, Who can be saved?, is "everyone!" This thrills me because I do certainly need to be saved.

How? Not by the Law of Moses.

The second question is How? How can a person be saved? Well, the Jews had the law, a great advantage. Moses had taught them how to live. Surely, they could boast across the Hellenized world that they had the way to salvation. On the contrary, Paul wrote, "For no human being will be justified in his sight by deeds prescribed by the law, for through the law comes the knowledge of sin" (Rom 3:20). Neither the law nor Moses will get me saved. The law can show me that I need to be saved. Moses can help me buy into the fact that all have sinned and need to be saved.

You ask, How can I be saved? Not by the law of Moses!

How Then?

How then can I be saved? Paul said, "But now, apart from law, the righteousness of God has been disclosed, and is attested by the law and the prophets, the righteousness of God through faith in Jesus Christ for all who believe" (Rom 3:21–22). According to the grammar of this setting, that word "righteousness" is the remedy for sin. It is what the sinner needs. It is salvation.

This one Greek word means "right, just, and fair." Try to keep all those connotations in mind when you see or hear the word. Seemingly, there is a God-provided way to be right, just, and fair apart from trying to do good deeds according to the law. And this God-provided way is through faith and trust in Jesus. It is a free gift by grace.

The Text

In the next chapter, I will tell you how long and how much I personally fought this teaching. We will ponder how a right, just, and fair God could come even close to acquitting me and still be right, just, and fair. And we will bring Abraham on stage. We have so much to talk about yet.

Let us reread the text in Rom 3, from which I have ellipted some of the repetitions:

> Now we know that, whatever the law says, it speaks to those who are under the law, so that every mouth may be silenced and the whole world may be held accountable to God. For 'no human being will be justified in his sight' by deeds prescribed by the law, for through the law comes the knowledge of sin. . . .
>
> But now, apart from the law, the righteousness of God has been disclosed and is attested by the law and the prophets, the righteousness of God through faith in Jesus Christ for all who believe. For there is no distinction, since all have sinned and fall short of the glory of God; they are now justified by his grace as a gift, through the redemption that is in Christ Jesus, . . .
>
> Then what becomes of boasting? It is excluded. By what law? By that of works? No, but by the law of faith. For we hold that a person is justified by faith apart from works prescribed by the law. . . . Do we then overthrow the law by this faith? By no means! On the contrary, we uphold the law. (Rom 3:19–24, 27–28, 31)

ABRAHAM AND ME, ROM 4:1-5, 13-17

Illustration and Review

I was not a smooth swimmer. Mostly I was afraid. I could go out into the deep water, of course, but my kick was more frantic than purposeful, my hands were more flail than fin, and I never could open my eyes underwater. I remember the lakes where I swam as a child. I can remember coming in from the deep, kicking and flailing hard, hoping I will make it. Seems like a long way. I am not breathing in sync with anything, just gasping whenever. Keep kicking, I tell myself. Keep kicking. And then, wonder of wonders, there is the floor beneath my feet. The sand comes up to meet me. I quit kicking and I find I am home free!

This is one of my illustrations of what I think I mean when saying that salvation is by faith. I need to quit kicking and discover that the sought-after goal is already at my feet. The feeling at that moment is what I want you to know.

In the previous chapter, we introduced the Roman Empire, which in Paul's time stretched all around the Mediterranean Sea and even as far north as the British Isles. The Roman Empire took over the Greek Empire after winning at Macedon in 168 BCE. Yet it was the Greek culture that the Romans assumed and spread; thus, you could be a Roman citizen and a Greek philosopher or artist at the same time. The epistle of Paul to the Romans is written in the midst of Greek culture to those who lived in the city of Rome, the capital of the Roman Empire. When Paul in this letter mentions Greeks or gentiles, he means the same thing by the two words, anyone who is not a Jew.

On the other hand, Jews were those who traced their lineage through Moses and Abraham back to Adam. They had the law, given them by Moses, and they considered themselves better than others because they could live according to the law.

Last time we heard Paul tell the lovers of the law that doing according to the law will not save them, that God has made a new and different way, that of faith in Jesus. He said neither Jews nor Greeks were actually doing according to the law. He established that Jews and gentiles alike are sinners. We cannot be saved by the law because we cannot keep the law. The law merely points out the fact that we need something better, and the better way is trusting Jesus.

It feels sort of like "Stand up now. Stop kicking."

It feels like my brother packing the bales on the hay wagon as I drove the tractor carefully around the hayfield, trying not to jerk and bump. He filled the wagon as full as possible and grabbed one more bale, standing on top of the stack, holding that last bale, and motioned me toward the barn. He never put that last fifty-pound bale down, and when we pulled into the barn, he threw that bale into the hay mow without ever having let it go. I asked him why he carried that heavy bale all the way in. He said, "I had the wagon packed so full, I didn't want to load it up any heavier."

No, that story did not happen because my brother had more common sense than that. Then, where is my common sense that would let go of my heavy load of sin, regret, and strenuous effort to get and keep myself right, just, and fair? When I realize God is carrying me and my load anyway, I can drop it all on God. I can trust God to sort out what God wants to handle, and to take care of the rest, too, maybe through me, maybe in other ways, however God wants to.

Abraham

Now we view Abraham, brought on stage by Paul in chapter 4 of his letter to the Romans. Paul said, "Abraham believed God, and that trust was marked to his account as righteousness" (Rom 4:3). Paul did not say that the faith made Abraham right, just, and fair. Nor did he suggest that Abraham was from then on right, just, and fair. Paul went on to do some more clarification of his own. This marking to Abraham's account was not done as wages for work done, it was not something due to Abraham; instead, it was a pure gift. The gift is given within a trusting relationship, trusting that God gives where nothing is due.

The part of Paul's logic that we did not read this time cites the Jewish ritual of circumcision. By the time of Paul, circumcision was important as an identifier of the Jewish race, something that set them apart from, and better than or more favored by God than, the uncircumcised, and even as the only ones who could receive God's favor. Paul often used the word "circumcision" to mean those who follow the law and do the deeds of the law. This is the word's first instance in Romans. The word had its original Bible setting in Abraham's story.

God asked Abraham to circumcise himself, his teen son Ishmael, and all the males in his camp. Every boy born thereafter was to be circumcised on the eighth day of his life. This was to be a sign to Abraham to help him each moment to remember the promise of God and his own inability to bring about that promise. By the time of Paul, the Jews had taken circumcision to a new level, a sign to God and everyone else that the Jews deserved God's favor more than others. Paul's comments single out the fact that Abraham's account was fixed for righteousness, justice, and fairness before he ever knew about circumcision. The resulting logic is that Abraham is the father of all who have faith, the uncircumcised as well as the circumcised. Abraham was counted right, just, and fair through faith, not through the law.

You will remember the Jews also depended heavily on being the descendants of Abraham. Both Jesus and Paul undermined that particular boast. Jesus said, "You've got to be born again" (John 3:3, author paraphrase), and Paul said, "Abraham is your father if you believe in Jesus" (Rom 4:16; 9:8, author paraphrase).

This was hard news for me. By my late teens I had done the law all my days. I lived by the law, by everything anyone even hinted was the will of God. Also, I was born right. If anyone has parents who could get them into heaven by trying, that was my parents. Paul denied that either works of the law or right ancestors will get me saved.

Me

In my late teens, I began to suspect that my works and my birth were not good enough, and maybe never could be good enough. I found out that mistakes and shortfalls dogged my days and, much as I wanted to fix me, my trying to do so was not working. Someone helped me to Romans, and I read it. I read Romans in *The Living Bible*, the simplest Bible I had available at that time. It seemed God was asking me to give up trying to be right, just, and fair.

One person said it was as if I had been trying to fly, out on the runway flapping my arms, until I was exhausted. Finally, maybe I was ready to decide that I could stop flapping my arms and get on a plane.

Somehow that did not seem at all fair to me. I said, "I got myself into this mess; I'd better get myself out." And under my breath I said, "But what if I can't?" I said, "I don't want to call on God to do something so unfair as to let me off, traitor that I am."

Something whispered, "God can do this and still be right, just, and fair because of Jesus' death (Rom 3:6). Just believe it." I reasoned, if it was simply that Jesus died in my place, I did not think that was fair, either. If it was that he died to show me how to live, well, I was ready to die, too, but living was a puzzle for which I could find no clue. I wanted God to save me from making mistakes. I wanted God to make me good because I thought God needed me good in order to use me. My angst was over hurting and disappointing God, others, and myself. I wanted God to make me stop disappointing people. I did not want to stop trying to be good, oh no, what horrible mistakes might I make if I stopped trying not to!

Furthermore, somehow, I came to know during those months of intense fighting with God, the long reach of this decision into my life. If I really buy into the good news that we are saved by faith in Jesus Christ and that this is by the free gift of God, paid for by absolutely nothing I did or can do, then there are some things I don't get to do. I don't get to be sure that something I do will not turn out to have been a mistake. I don't even get to know for sure the depths of what I might devise to depend on in the place of Christ sometime in the future, thus slapping his face rather than trusting him. I don't get to claim God on my side, because the closer I get to God the more falling short I see myself to be.

Since even I don't know my own depths, there are some things about others that I don't get to do. I don't get to go about as if I know God's will for someone else. I don't get to depend totally on pastors or elders for God's blessing or direction in my life. I don't get to spend my energies trying to figure out why someone did what they did. I don't get to know whether or not a certain person will be in heaven.

There are a lot of things I agree not to know if I buy into Paul's gospel of being right, just, and fair by believing in Jesus. I agree to live in less certainty, less "God is on my side" rhetoric, and without using fear, guilt, or shame as motivators for myself or others. Even if I am a leader and must place people in responsibilities, I do not get to judge motives, but only fruit, and I do not get to settle into thinking that my decisions are mistake-proof.

The cost is large for making this decision to trust God to take care of making me right, just, and fair. I fought it for months. When at last I gave it all to God, I had peace. There is nothing like this peace. This peace does not guarantee that I will always do things right and thereby earn opportunities and accolades on earth. This peace does not mean I will never have to cry and apologize over the ways I hurt others. This peace only guarantees that these are God's responsibilities and fully handled by God's love and grace.

The Text

My being right, just, and fair is like the loaves of bread I had ready to put in the oven. The yeast had risen the bread beautifully to high rounded tops. I had the oven set right. I set the tins on the racks gently. I closed the oven door gently. Then, instead of leaving the oven to do its work, I peeked incessantly and, after one of those peeks, I let go of the oven door and it slammed itself shut. Well, the bread fell. It had sticky dough in some places, and big holes in other places. It was fit for the ducks and the birds. I did not make the decision to leave the baking to the oven.

Paul wrote in our text, Rom 4:

> What then are we to say was gained by Abraham, our ancestor according to the flesh? For if Abraham was justified by works, he has something to boast about, but not before God. For what does the scripture say? 'Abraham believed God, and it was reckoned to him as righteousness.' Now to one who works, wages are not reckoned as a gift but as something due. But to one who without works trusts him who justifies the ungodly, such faith is reckoned as righteousness. . . .
>
> For the promise that he would inherit the world did not come to Abraham or to his descendants through the law but through the righteousness of faith. If it is the adherents of the law who are to be the heirs, faith is null and

the promise is void. For the law brings wrath, but where there is no law, neither is there violation.

For this reason it depends on faith, in order that the promise may rest on grace, and be guaranteed to all his descendants, not only to the adherents of the law but also to those who share the faith of Abraham. (Rom 4:1–5, 13–17)

ADAM AND ME, ROM 5:1, 6–10, 15, 17–21

The Search for Patient Zero

How did you catch it? Each national CDC wants to know. The WHO wants to know. Handling infectious diseases requires tracking. Yet nobody knows who patient zero was in the coronavirus timeline. According to MSN, what was possibly the first case arose on November 17, 2019, in a fifty-five-year-old person from Hubei province, but the data is not complete or confirmed. The first case of COVID-19 that was reported to the WHO was reported on December 31, having been infected on December 8. Contrarily, Chinese social media sites show spikes in the incidence of words related to COVID-19, like "shortness of breath," at least more than one week before the reported dates.[7]

Now suppose you were the person, or even suspected you might be the person, with whom the virus morphed or jumped and became a human plague. That would hurt! That would bend me over in pain for the whole world. I would watch the mounting deaths and disruptions with excruciating horror, even if it was not really my fault, even if I had no malicious intent, nor even had any way of knowing this was the moment the virus would jump the line and loose itself on the world. Even if I could not have stopped it, I would still be filled with horror.

Adam released a monster virus on this earth, and Paul calls us to consider Adam.

We have been in Romans long enough to realize that Paul called on deep Jewish history to make his point. Paul traversed this

7. Scher, "First COVID-19 Case."

entire history in his logic. We considered what Paul had to say about Moses and the law in response to the questions, Who can be saved, and how? We learned that Jews and all others can be saved, but not by the law. We considered what Paul had to say about Abraham and his descendants in response to the questions, Who can be saved, and how? We learned that Abraham's descendants and all others can be saved, but not by being his descendants and not by keeping the law even to the point of being circumcised. This time we consider what Paul had to say about Adam and Jesus in response to the questions, Who can be saved, and how? We will learn that, though Adam released the virus of sin and death on all his descendants, Jesus released grace into the world. Jesus released a free gift of life in restored relationship with God. Jesus released the cure.

Adam

What did Adam do that released the monster virus? Paul said of Adam's descendants, "All have sinned" (Rom 3:23). Everyone has the virus. All of us are carriers and pass it on to others every day. Even if our sin does not look exactly like Adam's, or just like each other's, even if I cannot claim to know how you sin, or that my sin is not as desperate as yours, we all, every one of us, have the virus.

What did Adam do that released this monster virus? Oh, he ate the fruit. What did that do? Paul did not say. No one in the Bible gives a completely satisfactory answer to the question of what exactly Adam did that upset the universe. Scholars write papers about it. Preachers pontificate on it. Mommies say what mommies say while little children ponder. I do not have the answer. However, I think we will wander down a few imaginary thought pathways, call them metaphors, to try to understand what Adam did and what Jesus did.

Think of what happened as if a carjacker knocked on Adam's car door, and Adam opened the door. The car is this world.

Think of what happened as if a coup overthrew the real God of this world. This coup was made possible because Adam, its president, switched sides.

Think of what happened as if a virus jumped species because Adam gave it a favorable environment.

Think of what happened as if a tyrant conquered new territory and made oppressive and killing laws. Adam was the first sycophant and adapter.

Think of what happened as if a puppeteer went small and was swallowed by the puppet. Adam had all his children born within the puppet's belly. Then the puppet turned out to have a mean mind of its own.

We are hopelessly born and adapted on the enemy's ground, within the enemy's system, thinking the enemy's thoughts, dreaming of the enemy's dangling carrot and other toys. We know nothing else. Our world is a closed system; it is all we have. We are all sinners!

Jesus

Paul said, "While we were still sinners, Christ died for us" (Rom 5:8). There is no better news anywhere. "Christ died for the ungodly" (Rom 5:6). This is the only hope on the horizon for me. Rarely might someone die for a good person, and there was no chance of my being good enough to save. There still is no chance of that.

Yet while I was a sinner, Christ died for me, and Christ died for the ungodly.

What did Jesus do that released this grace and gift in the world? Oh, he died. What did that do? Paid my debt? Took my punishment? Influenced the world for healing and morality? Proved the enduring status of God's law? Gave us an example? Somehow no answer does it all, and yet so many different answers have pieces of the hope. The simple fact for Paul was that Christ died for the ungodly and by his blood, counted me before God to be right, just, and fair.

Paul went on here to say that Jesus will finish what he started in you and me. "Much more surely then, now that we have been justified by his blood, will we be saved through him from the wrath of God. . . . much more surely, having been reconciled, will we be saved by his life" (Rom 5:9–10). Since the Greek word behind "saved," is often translated "healed," our metaphor of needing healing from a virus is proved appropriate. Being "saved" is a total restoration to health and relationship. As surely as Jesus rose from the dead, so surely will he finish the work in us.

Please, most esteemed reader, let us work together to take in Paul's astonishing statements, and know that somehow you and I are made right with God the moment we believe it. I do not have to figure out how God did it or does it. All I need to do is imagine the statements he makes and let them sink in.

> For if the many died through the one man's trespass, much more surely have the grace of God and the free gift in the grace of the one man, Jesus Christ, abounded for the many" (Rom 5:15).
>
> For the judgment following one trespass brought condemnation, but the free gift following many trespasses brings justification [that is, being made right, just, and fair]" (Rom 5:16).
>
> Just as by the one man's disobedience the many were made sinners, so by the one man's obedience the many will be made righteous [or right, just, and fair]" (Rom 5:19).
>
> Just as sin exercised dominion in death, so grace might also exercise dominion through justification [being made right, just, and fair], leading to eternal life through Jesus Christ our Lord" (Rom 5:21).
>
> "While we were still sinners, Christ died for us." (Rom 5:8)
>
> "Christ died for the ungodly" (Rom 5:6).

I tell you today that Jesus is the cure for the monster virus that Adam loosed.

Me

I used to wish intensely that I could have been like the thief on the cross and die the moment after I believed. Instead, I was made to live days and weeks and years after that, making mistake after mistake, falling short of what I knew over and over again, and feeling that I was only a parasite on God's earth. After fighting with God for months, I realized I really could die but in a different way. Admitting that I am the ungodly one for whom Jesus died is sort of like dying, dying to all those dreams of unassailable reputation and praiseworthy service in the world. I could admit that my life is unmanageable. I could believe that Jesus could restore me to sanity. I could make a decision to turn my will and my life over to his care.[8] This then, is what I find to be faith: I cannot, he can, and I decide to let him.

Faith was mentioned back when we were talking about Moses and the law being unable to save us, but it is by the faith of Jesus that we are saved (Rom 3:22, 26). This formulation, "the faith of Jesus," is used quite often in the New Testament. The preposition in Greek could yield either "faith in Jesus" or "faith of Jesus," and scholars love to write long tomes of arguments proving one or the other. Is it solely some kind of faith Jesus had back then? Or is it my faith in Jesus that saves me, even if that faith is placed in me by Jesus? I want you to feel both meanings whenever you come across the phrase, "the faith of Jesus." The new way to right, just, and fair character is through faith or trust in who Jesus is and what Jesus has done for us, *and* it is also through the faith that Jesus had in his Father's good willingness to save, this being the same faith Jesus has placed in you by the Holy Spirit.

And here's a caution. It will never do you or me good to start examining our faith as if our faith is what saves us. Some say, "I don't think my faith is strong enough." Or "Look, I made this mistake. My faith must not be good enough." Or "I'll need to work on my faith before I can have God's gift of salvation." If I say this, I have only substituted my work of faith for the old kind of "my works." This is extremely easy for me to slip into. I find something that worked in making me feel able to grasp the free gift of salvation, and then I focus on repeating or increasing that thing or process or thought rather than always focusing on Christ. It is a given we humans will do that. For this reason, I have to refocus continually my pondering

---

8. Anonymous, *Alcoholics Anonymous*, 59.

onto Jesus rather than anything else, my faith, my sins, or persons I have hurt.

The Text

Of the three Bible characters Paul cited in his argument in Romans, Adam is the least popular but is used most by Paul to highlight what Jesus did. You see, in the whole Bible, Moses' name gets 783 mentions. Abraham's gets 230, and Adam's gets a small 31 citations. I suppose all who might have cited Adam knew of his complicity in the hijacking of our world and refrained from citing the story of a traitor. I figure if Adam can be saved, if Adam can be made right, just, and fair, then there must be hope for me, and I think we have been finding some of that hope in Romans.

Let us read again our text from Rom 5.

> Therefore, since we are justified by faith, we have peace with God through our Lord Jesus Christ, . . .
> For while we were still weak, at the right time Christ died for the ungodly. Indeed, rarely will anyone die for a righteous person—though perhaps for a good person someone might actually dare to die. But God proves his love for us in that while we still were sinners Christ died for us. Much more surely then, now that we have been justified by his blood, will we be saved through him from the wrath of God. For if while we were enemies, we were reconciled to God through the death of his Son, much more surely, having been reconciled, will we be saved by his life. . . .
> But the free gift is not like the trespass. For if the many died through the one man's trespass, much more surely have the grace of God and the free gift in the grace of the one man, Jesus Christ, abounded for the many. . .
> If, because of the one man's trespass, death exercised dominion through that one, much more surely will those who receive the abundance of grace and the free gift of righteousness exercise dominion in life through the one man, Jesus Christ.

> Therefore, just as one man's trespass led to condemnation for all, so one man's act of righteousness leads to justification and life for all. For just as by the one man's disobedience the many were made sinners, so by the one man's obedience the many will be made righteous. But law came in, with the result that the trespass multiplied, but where sin increased, grace abounded all the more, so that, just as sin exercised dominion in death, so grace might also exercise dominion through justification leading to eternal life through Jesus Christ our Lord. (Rom 5:1, 6–10, 15, 17–21)

GET LIFE IN MY LIFE, ROM 7:18—8:14

Review and Disclaimers

Now I want to pull together our past work in the first five chapters in Romans, with a couple quick surveys of Rom 6 and Rom 7, to give us images and definitions by which to reread Rom 8.

Let me make a couple disclaimers first.

I know I am reading Paul through my own experience. I figure, what else can I do? Paul's statements about his not having attained, and doing what he does not want to do, are pieces of gold to me. I believe he can be in Christ, confident in God's salvation, while still knowing his own shortcomings and mistakes. The closer he came to Christ, the more sinful he saw himself to be. It is a conundrum and paradox, but I think of it as two sides of the same coin. Death and resurrection are two sides of the same weekend. Giving up and audacious confidence live in me, both at the same time. If I preach only one, I preach heresy, yet I preach heresy every time I preach, because I am too small to get it all in one sermon.

When I preach, you get only half the picture, or less. I hope you come back and back and back, as I have to come back and back and back to the Bible and Jesus, to learn more. I am told even the angels desire to study this (1 Pet 1:12); therefore, I expect I will be doing so for eternity.

I will not know when I am done here on earth. The closer I get to Him the more shortfall I see in myself. My solution is to repent, surrender, and give it up, again, to be covered in Christ's forgiveness and righteousness. I myself do not even know all the ways I can devise against trusting God.

Yet simply trusting God with all of this is a joyful experience, worth everything it seems to cost me. It is definitely a two-sided coin, this death and life at the same time, both sides growing more and more intense, stretching my heart with more space to know him, I guess.

With those disclaimers in place, now we will pull together our past work in the first five chapters of Romans, with a couple quick surveys of Rom 6 and Rom 7, to give us images and definitions by which to reread Rom 8.

Dying with Jesus, Rom 6

In Rom 6, Paul cited baptism as evidence that what is required is dying with Jesus. He had spent the first five chapters proving to us that we are all sinners and cannot escape that condition by anything we might devise or do. He cited practices of those who do not worship the God of the Jews and practices of those who do worship the God of the Jews. He cited Moses, the giver of the law but not the savior of our lives, Abraham who was counted righteous before anyone could have kept the law of Moses, and Adam the one man by whom came all this tragedy called sin as contrasted with Christ the one man who brought the answers. Then in Rom 6, Paul named the solution: dying with Jesus. That is right, dying is the only way to be free from sin and free to follow Jesus in life.

This is the good death, giving up in or with Jesus. This is the death that puts life in my life. Paul said, "You also must consider yourselves dead to sin and alive to God in Christ Jesus" (Rom 6:11).

Now we will review some images we mentioned last week of this dying with Jesus.

It is like swimming to shore, feeling the sand under your body, and realizing you can stop kicking now. Your kicking can die.

It is like my brother stacking the bales high then climbing up for the ride to the barn, while carrying one huge bale in his strong arms all the way in. Not! No, he always let the wagon carry the bale and himself. He let his own strength die for the ride to the barn.

It is like me giving up on my efforts to fly by flapping my arms, which giving up allows me to go into the airport and let a plane carry me. My flapping dies.

It is like me putting the perfectly risen loaves of bread in the oven only to check on them every other minute. Not! I will let the oven do its work. My opening the oven dies.

It is like me saying, "God, take the wheel," and then grabbing at the wheel at the most dangerous parts of the drive, or like me continually jumping out to push. Not! Indeed, very often in real life I try to help God by trying to be good. My trying to be good can die.

Staying Dead with Jesus, Rom 7

In Rom 7, Paul presents several conundrums all consumed with the one conundrum: How are we to go on living if we are dead? Paul writes this section in a style that proves he is describing conundrums. His words seem to take us around in circles. Before we read now, I want to review some new words we have brought in to translate some of Paul's Greek words.

"Righteous" means right, just, and fair. (I want us to think of all of these connotations with this word.)

"Faith" is trusting friendship with God or trusting as children of God.

"Sin" is the place I live without God, without faith, without trusting God. It is a physical space, a psychological space, and a spiritual space, all without God.

Law 1 denotes the way things are, the condition, or usual action, of things, in gravity, in my mind, in the Spirit, in sin and death.

Law 2 denotes God's commands given by Moses or Jesus, the Ten Commandments, love one another, etc. You can tell the difference in Paul's meaning between these two uses of law, by the context.

Saved without Swords

Death 1 is good death, giving up in and with Jesus. It gets life in my life.

Death 2 is ugly death, giving up without Jesus. It gets death in my life, and then eternal death.

Flesh means trying to do in my own strength.

Unfortunately, the King James Version of the Bible further confused the use of this word "flesh" by sometimes, but not always, translating it with the word "carnal," with the result that I grew up hearing preaching against the "carnal nature" and the "fleshly lusts." I had no idea how to accomplish their death except by suicide. Now I know that the words "carnal" and "flesh" translate the same Greek word and refer to my using my own strength to try to keep the law and be good enough. This was life-changing for me.

Now we are ready to read Paul in Rom 7:

> For I know that nothing good dwells within me, that is, in my [trying to do in my own strength]. I can will what is right, but I cannot do it. For I do not do the good I want, but the evil I do not want is what I do. Now if I do what I do not want, it is no longer I that do it, but [the place I live without God] that dwells within me. So I find it to be a [way things are] that when I want to do what is good, evil lies close at hand. For I delight in the [law of God] in my inmost self, but I see in my members another [way things are] at war with [the way things are] in my mind, making me captive to [the way things are] in [the place I live without God] that dwells in my members. What a wretched person I am! Who will rescue me from this [trying to do in my own strength] of [ugly death]? Thanks be to God through Jesus Christ our Lord! So then, with my mind I am a slave to the [law of God,] but with my [trying to do in my own strength] I am a slave to [the way things are] in [the place I live without God]. (Rom 7:18–25)

It is like I have continually to stop kicking in order to trust Jesus and stand up.

It is like I have to continue to restrain myself from picking up that bale of hay to carry it myself while Jesus carries both me and my burden.

It is like I have to remember to remind myself to stop flapping my arms to fly to release myself to trust Jesus and rest in his arms on the journey.

It is like I have to distract myself by looking to Jesus so as not to be continually opening the oven door to check on my progress.

It is like my driver has to let me get my bumps and scrapes sometimes to cause me to remember not to get out and push while Jesus is driving.

Living with Jesus, Rom 8

I still had a problem. Unlike the thief on the cross, I have to go on living after giving up to Jesus. "Dying with Jesus" and "Living for Jesus" are two wonderful old hymns, though they created an incomprehensible conundrum for me at this time.[9]

I heard about what a person should become in Jesus. I heard that after being made right, just, and fair, I had to go on to where I would end up actually being right, just, and fair, and not have to be made that way anymore. I heard that I should not have to do any more dying but should be living for Jesus now instead. And I kept on being blindsided by my own mistakes!

I heard over and over again about striving to be good, to please God, and to make it through the narrow way. Then I read Romans. Over and over again I read Romans. Now I firmly believe and testify to you that the finishing that God wants to do in me is more of the same that God already began in me (Phil 1:6; Heb 12:1; Col 2:6; Rom 1:17). At every new opportunity and adventure, I am to learn again to give it up and turn my life over to Jesus, then watch what he will do. At every new turn and decision, I am to recognize again my life is unmanageable by me, and humbly bow to God's management. At every new discovery of my own deep betrayals and shortfalls, I am to take them as proof that I am a person Jesus came to save when he came to save the ungodly. This is what my mistakes are for, the same as the law, to bring me back to surrender to God.

---

9. Whittle, "Dying with Jesus"; Chisholm, "Living for Jesus."

Then, you ask, "Where is the joy? If I must continually die, then where is the life?"

Oh, my dear friends, please try it. You will find there is the highest joy and living in the dying. They are two sides of the same page, two events of the same weekend for Jesus. They must happen simultaneously, the always-dying with Jesus and the living with Jesus, surrender and great big vision, both of them growing more and more intense through time, stretching out heart-spaces for God!

I am not saved by checking to see if my repentance or my faith is good enough. I am not saved by being good enough—ever, not in my youth, not in my senior years, not on the first day of my walk with God, not on the day I die, and not on a single day in the eternal future. I am not ever saved by being good enough at anything.

Mind you, what God wants to do in and through me might be good beyond all my imagination, good beyond all the preachers' pontifications, good beyond all comprehension on my own. I hope I learn to keep from pushing the car to let him drive me wherever and however far at whatever speed he wants to.

The Text

Now we will read the scripture from Rom 8. We will use the definitions we created in the previous section. I would have us notice also that in this reading, it seems to me that Paul uses the names God, Jesus, and Spirit in somewhat interchangeable ways.

> There is therefore now no condemnation for those who are in Christ Jesus. For [the way things are] in the Spirit of life in Christ Jesus has set you free from [the way things are] in [the place you live without God] and in [ugly death.] For God has done what the [law of God,] weakened by the [trying to do in my own strength,] could not do: by sending his own Son in the likeness of [trying to do in my own strength,] and to deal with [the place I live without God,] he condemned [the place I live without God] in the [trying to do in my own strength,] so that the just requirement of the [law of God] might be fulfilled in us, who walk not according to the [trying to

do in our own strength] but according to the Spirit. For those who live according to the [trying to do in their own strength] set their minds on the things of the [trying to do in their own strength,] but those who live according to the Spirit set their minds on the things of the Spirit. To set the mind on the [trying to do in my own strength] is [ugly death], but to set the mind on the Spirit is life and peace. For this reason the mind that is set on the [trying to do in my own strength] is hostile to God; it does not submit to [God's law]—indeed it cannot, and those who are in the [trying to do in their own strength] cannot please God.

But you are not in the [trying to do in your own strength]; you are in the Spirit, since the Spirit of God dwells in you. Anyone who does not have the Spirit of Christ does not belong to him. But if Christ is in you, though the [trying to do in your own strength] is [good dead] because of [the place you live without God,] the Spirit is life because of [righteousness, justice, and fairness]. If the Spirit of him who raised Jesus from the [good death] dwells in you, he who raised Christ from the [good death] will give life to your mortal bodies also through his Spirit that dwells in you.

So then, brothers and sisters, we are debtors, not to the [trying to do in our own strength], to live according to the [trying to do in our own strength]—for if you live according to the [trying to do in your own strength,] you will [ugly die]; but if by the Spirit you put to [good death] the deeds of the [trying to do in your own strength,] you will live. For all who are led by the Spirit of God are children of God. (Rom 8:1–14)

HE IS MINE! ROM 8:28, 31–39

Music for a Minute

"I am safe in You | She is safe in You | He is safe in You | We are safe in You."

These are lyrics to the first verse I have written to Bach's "Two Part Invention #14 in Bb." I invite you to put this book down and go listen to this Bach piece now. I suggest you look online for one of the slower renditions so you can hear distinctly the four-plus-one repeated figures in the music.[10] It will be more fun for you if you get this song in your head now.

Welcome back! I hope you enjoyed the music. I hope you also notice at least three things about the music itself as we get started now.

One, there is a moment when solo gives way to duet, a moment when harmony joins the experience, creating a lift and expansion in the listener's engagement and enjoyment.

Two, the theme is pushed along by delightful little baskets, that is, four quicker notes moving down and then up or inverted to up then down. These baskets are carried by one in solo, passed back and forth in handoff or canon, and then lifted high by duet in close harmony.

Three, a theme of safety can be felt, implied, I think, by the covering chord work during the making of most of those little baskets.

Let us study the little baskets for a moment. I made some simple lyrics to go with the four plus one figure. Here is the initiating solo. Hear it as if with a beautifully resonant voice. "I am safe in You | She is safe in You | He is safe in You | We are safe in You | Hear our prayer, O Lord | This is what we pray."

Here the baskets are passed back and forth energetically between two voices in prayer. "Help us love our friends | Guard and keep them safe | Help us see the ones | We have pushed away | Be amid us, Lord | Let Your presence stay | Let Your presence grow."

That much would be a beautiful message for our time of holding in check our anxiety and fear in the face of "stay at home" and "shelter in place" orders and wondering about future quarantines and curfews and lockdowns and martial presence. Let us use this music and our highest work in Romans to help us into peace and joy in this time.

---

10. E.g., Jane's Piano Tutorial, "Bach Two-Part Invention No. 14 Piano Tutorial."

However, a minor sound infiltrates our music while the two voices each make two baskets before handing them off, trading intertwined ideas. "I am feeling lost | I defend myself | Louder all the time | Lost in argument | Feel betrayed, alone | Meaning gone, depressed."

Given all this, I am ready and eager for the central highlights of the music, the canon, or round, and then the duet. First, hear these two voices singing, a little basket with a glorious extended melody, at the same time while always answering each other. "Will You shepherd us—back to You | You are with us now—You see us | Please forgive and heal—hurts we've caused | Bring forgiveness bought—on the cross."

Can you hear the soul-thrilling harmony? The sound gets inside me and lifts my inner being into breathless joy. And there's more.

Now the little baskets, of four notes plus one, are made by two voices together in the closest harmony. They skip and dance at the height of exuberance and the lift already present inside me expands the limits of my endurance. "We are safe in You | Found, we're safe in You | One, we're safe in You | May Your favor shine | May Your grace abound | May Your peace remain | May Your kingdom come | Let Your will be done | Heaven on this earth | When Your time is come."

After this climax, the best thing to do is to intermingle and handoff from one voice to another the beautiful desire, still always in the lovely little baskets, repeating the words of the climax and finishing with a glorious triumph. "You will shepherd us | You are with us now | You will help us love | You will keep us safe | We are safe in You."

Somehow the safety celebrated in the lyrics seems ultra-safe when joined to excellent music.

All Things Work Together for Good, Rom 8:28–30

I hope and pray that your experience with Romans is somewhat like the renditions of our musical selection. I want you to feel the lift and joy of that to which we are coming, of being able to say with me without a shadow of doubt, "He is mine!" After Paul introduced his topic, he cited various heroes of the Old Testament in clear tones, full of the resonance resulting from years of telling and re-telling. This was like the solo part. Then Paul brought out into our hearing the intertwining of death and life, and the soul-soaring solutions provided in the two sides of the same weekend, of Christ's death and resurrection. That is the minor sound in the music and the canon of two voices yearningly intertwined.

In this chapter, we enter the fabulous lift of the duet, where what we have in Jesus must be celebrated in every breath. Hear it: "We know that all things work together for good for those who love God, who are called according to his purpose" (Rom 8:28). This is the first buzz of the climax of the song. "We know that all things work together for good for those who love God, who are called according to his purpose," those who can say, "he is mine."

It is hard to see COVID-19 working for the good. And then there are the layoffs, the loss of income. Some will lose businesses, or retirement funds. Many will die.

Oh, my friends, there is something we do know. We know that all things work for good. We know it deeply because it is part of our trust in God. And we know this has to do with all things.

When I was in first grade, my mother taught school and had to go to meetings in the evenings. My father drove a truck and was out of town. Though my brother was in the next room, I never thought of connecting with him in my fear. I was most afraid our house would burn down while my mother was away. She taught me to look out the window and, if I did not see any red glow in the sky, I could know the house was not burning. She taught me something else, too. She started me on a path of trusting God enough to say that if God allowed the house to burn, then it would be within God's will, and I really would not want anything outside of God's will, now would I? This is the rock bottom foundation of my trust in these times of COVID-19.

I had another, more difficult problem with Rom 8:28. I could not keep myself from my burning questions. What if I don't love God enough? What if all of what I think is loving God is from selfish motives? What if I don't love God? What if I am not called according to his purpose? And the next two verses did not help, remaining very confusing to me, talking about foreknowledge, predestination, calling, justification, and glorification. Some said these were steps I had to take.

No, my friends, please look again. Whatever else they may be, these works are all done by God and not by me! I give up on trying to make all these happen. I trust my salvation in God's hands! I simply love and say yes to God, simply—and I can know for sure that all things work together for good for me, for others, and for the advancement of God's kingdom. The closer I come to Jesus, the more disastrous I see my own trying to do in my own strength, the more I recognize insecurities and addictions in myself, and that is where God welcomes me. He saves the ungodly, the un-good, and I may never see or recognize the good He works in and through me. The fact that he is mine is everything to me.

The Spirit of God has the right and ability to make me love and desire holiness, to shape my character after the holy law of God, to use my passion for Him as witness to many or few. What God will make of me is not my concern. I must stay in repentance and forgiveness, in dying and living with Jesus. Herein, in the conjunction of dying and living, lies my incredible happiness.

He is mine!

Nothing Can Separate Us from God's Love, Rom 8:31–39

Paul was pacing the courtroom. He had made a brilliant argument, citing evidence from Moses, Abraham, Adam, Jesus, and himself. Now he made his most eloquent closing argument, persuading you and me to vote for Jesus, to acquit Jesus and God of all those insinuations and accusations that God means us harm, that God withholds good, that God's character is flawed toward harsh and unreasonable judgments.

Paul's closing argument was that nothing can separate us from the love of God. Nothing—not COVID-19, not death, not anything in life, not politics, not the media. Nothing—not imperfect faith, not insufficient repentance, not mistakes, not my own "trying in my own strength" that is hidden from me or not yet imagined. Nothing will be allowed to separate us from his love. God is for us, and no one can stand against us. Jesus intercedes for us and neither he nor anyone else will be allowed to condemn us. Nothing can separate us from the love of God. Paul shouts his conclusion. I join Paul in begging you to believe it.

Let us go through it again another way. Eugene Lowry has studied sermons and has noticed that many sermons have a plot much like a story. He identified narrative clues or steps to the plot.[11] We will now examine Paul's work in Romans as if it were narrative, looking for these clues.

First, there's the Oops! Something upsets the picture. In a crime novel, it might be the killing. In Romans, I think it is the puzzle Paul faces as to how non-Jews could be saved in the same way Jews are, introduced in Rom 1-2, and followed up later in Rom 9-12.

Second, there's the Ugh! The upset grows in scope and depth. In a crime novel, it might be the fleshing out of the characters or the timeline. In Romans, I think it is the citing of Moses, Abraham, Adam, and Jesus to show many facets of the problem of salvation, in Rom 3-5.

Third, there's the Aha! The core of the solution shows itself. In a crime novel, it might be the discovery of a smoking gun or a suicide note. In Romans, I think it is the use of baptism to show the importance of dying with Jesus and then the inefficacy of Paul's trying to do in his own strength, in Rom 6-7.

Fourth, there's the Whee! The solution expands to solve all issues. In a crime novel, it might be focused investigation of the new discovery. In Romans, I think it is the powerful description of life in the Spirit, that is a quality of life tasting of heaven, in Rom 8:1-14.

Fifth, there's the Yeah! or Yay! The consequences of the solution come into play and finally reach every character and every situation. In a crime novel, it might be a final scene or sequence that brings all characters together and shows their new position. In

---

11. Lowry, *Homiletical Plot*, 27-73.

Romans, I think it is this section of Rom 8:28–39. We know that all things work together for good for those who love God, and nothing, nothing at all, can separate us from the love of God. He is mine.

Rejoice with me! We can live in the Yay! today. Just as I can read a crime novel or Paul's argument all in one day, I need to hold gently in my hands the Oops! Ugh! Aha! Whee! And Yay! All of them in my life at once. The dying and the living. The cross and the resurrection. I can live today in the Yay! And tomorrow. And the next day. I can choose this moment to honor the whole narrative plot in my life, and I can choose the same thing the next moment under different pressures, and I can choose the same thing the moment after that, growing into new character as God opens up each moment.

He is mine!

The Text

Let us read it: the climactic music, the closing argument, the Yeah!, in Rom 8.

> We know that all things work together for good for those who love God, who are called according to his purpose.
> . . .
> What then are we to say about these things? If God is for us, who is against us? He who did not withhold his own Son, but gave him up for all of us, will he not with him also give us everything else? Who will bring any charge against God's elect? It is God who justifies. Who is to condemn? It is Christ Jesus, who died, yes, who was raised, who is at the right hand of God, who indeed intercedes for us.
> Who will separate us from the love of Christ? Will hardship, or distress, or persecution, or famine, or nakedness, or peril, or sword? . . .
> No, in all these things we are more than conquerors through him who loved us. For I am convinced that neither death, nor life, nor angels, nor rulers, nor things present, nor things to come, nor powers, nor height, nor depth, nor anything else in all creation, will be able

to separate us from the love of God in Christ Jesus our Lord. (Rom 8:28, 31–39)

He is mine!

WHO CAN BE SAVED, AND HOW? ROM 9:1–5, 30–32; 10:1–4, 12; 12:1–3, 16

Odd Salvations

Rahab was saved when the walls of her home city, Jericho, fell and the city burned. She became the wife of Salmon, the mother of Boaz, the mother-in-law to Ruth. Apparently, she and her family assimilated into the Israelite tribes as they grew to occupy Canaan (Josh 6:22–24).

Ruth was a Moabite, of the people who had treated Israel most treacherously years before on their way to Canaan, seducing them to fornication and idolatry and thereby into God's disfavor. Ruth was a loving and discrete girl. She became the wife of Boaz, the mother of Obed, and the grandmother of Jesse, who was father to David the king (Ruth 1–4).

Rahab and Ruth were invited into the community of God's specially-called people. Among themselves, according to God's promise, Israel was considered to be a privileged people.

Jonah was part of God's special people, and he did not like the people who lived in Nineveh (Jonah 1–4). They were a tough people. They were bullies. Jonah was happy with the message he was given by God to tell them, that they and their city would be destroyed within forty days. However, Jonah also had trouble with God. He figured God's compassion would win out and he would not carry through with the destruction. Jonah realized he was being sent to the city to save the people, not to taunt them with the coming destruction. Jonah saw that he would lose credibility no matter how he carried himself. That is why he took off down to Joppa by the sea, got on a boat going the opposite direction from that of Nineveh, and went to the bottom of the boat to sleep.

Maybe you know the story, how God used a storm and a big fish to get Jonah wakened and turned around. Jonah gave that message and the city repented and turned to God. God's compassion kicked in and he went to where Jonah was sitting on the hill, overlooking the city, waiting for the smoke to rise. Jonah screamed at God. This is why he had not wanted to come. God did it again, saved people who were not Israelites, these horrible, mean people who lived a very different way from how Jonah lived. God said, "I care about people I have made" (Jonah 4:10–11, author paraphrase).

Strange salvations. Odd salvations. These stories help us to ask, Who can be saved, and how? We have spent some time in Romans where Paul went to great lengths to show, first, that everyone has sinned and, second, that the law that came through Moses cannot help us. The banker, the busser, the six-timer prison inmate, the rich kid that buys his way out of prison, all have fallen short of the ideal. The preacher, the judge, and I, we have all sinned and are fit only for eternal separation from God. That is in Rom 1–3.

However! There is a "however"! Paul dove deep into Israel's history and theology to expound the "however."

God chose Abraham and promised to send a Messiah to save his descendants. God even promised to Adam that he would fix and turn around the horrible pact that Adam had made with the devil. This would require the death of God's Son and would be effective to turn off death. This is in Rom 4–5.

Then in Rom 6–8, Paul made the most audacious summary of how the believer dies and lives in Christ and can have a vibrant life full of trusting God in every circumstance. It is an essay unmatched for its imagery and celebration. I hope you will go back and read it again.

Here we finish examining Paul's letter to the Romans. It was not the Romans, however, that consumed his thoughts and purpose in these final chapters. It was the Israelites, his own people, who commanded his attention. His top question was, Can Jews be saved? If so, why did their leaders reject Jesus? We will discover the one factor that underlies all rejection of salvation and its results that permeate everything. Then we will seek to understand Paul's resolving conclusion about his people, the Jews. Some people call

SAVED WITHOUT SWORDS

Paul anti-Semitic because of these chapters in Romans. I will try to show you how Paul meant to talk to all of us in this chapter on Who can be saved, and how?

Why Do People Reject Being Saved?

We have no written record of Paul's family. Of mother, father, siblings, and cousins, we have nothing. Instead of family, Paul poured out of his great store of emotion for the churches he started. Here, we see those emotions come gushing forth for his people, the Israelites. He wrote, "I would give my own salvation to know that my people are saved. Israel has it all, the laws of God, the history with God, the promises. They were chosen by God to do a specific job, like the potter chooses a lump of clay that will suit his purpose for the piece he plans" (Rom 9:1–5, author paraphrase). Paul went on recounting some history stories about God's choice of Israel.

Do you know a nation or family that "has it all"? Have you ever remembered the beginning of your nation with a feeling of pride that God brought it forth? Is there anyone who could look at you and say you "have it all"? Paul was talking about his flesh and blood who had it made, not only in things and money but also in spiritual assurance. All they had to do was to mention Abraham or Moses and they were accepted into the spiritual giants' club. Though there were some left out, Paul was here writing about the privileged ones.

Paul wrote:

> What then are we to say? Gentiles, [people who are not Jews] who did not strive for righteousness, have attained it, that is, righteousness through faith; but Israel, who did strive for the righteousness that is based on the law, did not succeed in fulfilling that law. Why not? Because they did not strive for it on the basis of faith, but as if it were based on works.... Brothers and sisters, my heart's desire and prayer to God for them is that they may be saved. I can testify that they have a zeal for God, but it is not enlightened. For, being ignorant of the righteousness that comes from God, and seeking to establish their own, they have not submitted to God's righteousness.

> For Christ is the end of the law so that there may be righteousness for everyone who believes. . . . For there is no distinction between Jew and Greek [people who were not Jews]; the same Lord is Lord of all and is generous to all who call on him. (Rom 9:30–32; 10:1–4, 12)

Paul knew that his kin were zealous for God but ignorant of the free gift of God. Therefore, they went about trying to establish their own righteousness. Did you know that, while I go about trying to be good enough, I cannot be saved? I will not be able to submit to God's righteousness if I am guarding or reaching for my own righteousness, or reputation of righteousness.

Satan and sin have planted in each of us the craving to do something to assure our betterment. As long as this is our principle in life, we have no barrier against going all the way in sin. It is indeed a puzzle because working for our own betterment will likely keep us out of jail, in school, at the job, taking care of our family, and acquiring things for our security. Working hard for our own betterment will raise our reputation in the community and garner nice statements of our reliability. We can get addicted to these rewards.

Further, the shame and disdain piled on someone who does not work for his or her betterment is nearly unbearable. Even if a person has a legitimate illness or disability that keeps him or her from full endeavor, shame is passed around.

We carry all these reactions and interactions over into our relationship with God and we cannot stop ourselves either from the many little and even unnoticed ways in which we depend on ourselves rather than on God, or from the glaring moments we fail to trust and instead operate out of fear.

Perhaps you said, "Saved? What would I be saved from? I'm doing okay, just need to work a little harder." Or "I'll turn over a new leaf and go to church more. That will make me feel better." Or maybe you said, "You know, I don't need any downer people in my life who tell me I can't do something."

We go about to establish our own righteousness and totally fail to submit to the righteousness that comes by a faith relationship with God.

Saved without Swords

What Happens to a Person or a Society That Rejects Being Saved?

Let us follow this thought for a bit. Imagine it with me. A society that finds its salvation in work, in productivity and the necessarily resulting consumption and marketing, will find its attention filled with these interests besides further interests in transportation, communication, technology, and financial and other sectors of the economy. Walter Brueggemann writes, "The force of technology . . . has indeed produced a bubble of illusion, a totalizing environment of certitude, entitlement, and privilege. That enterprise renders the steadfastness of God irrelevant. It is remote from the weakness, foolishness, and poverty of Christ. Thus the urgency of the truth-telling of Jeremiah and Paul is immediately contemporary among us."[12] We may think we are the privileged ones while we consider God irrelevant and keep Jesus remote.

A person or family who holds to this principle of saving ourselves, or establishing our own righteousness by our own works, will perhaps have a great work ethic, but if there is a family member who does not work so well, he or she is likely to be worked over with persuasion and ridicule. If there is a person in the community who works hard in a different way from how the first family works, maybe no one will pay him or her for the artwork or the odd roles he or she fills. If there is a person in the community holding this principle, who had hard times in health or money, it would seem appropriate to blame that person for the hard times and not help him or her. If I hold the principle of saving myself by my own works, my life will be one endless cycle of works and I will try to foist that endless cycle on others, too. If given enough time and incentive, I will use coercion, fear, shame, and guilt to make people go my way, which of course I think is the best way.

There are whole institutions and societies, churches and nations that operate by the principle of saving oneself by doing. I believe these entities have no barrier against bringing coercion, fear, shame, and guilt into the operating culture of that organization.

---

12. Brueggemann, *Preaching Jeremiah*, 87.

Did you ask, "Why should I want to be saved? and from what should I be saved?"

This is the answer. I can be saved from the rat race of doing; that is my life. And when I am willing to submit to God's way of saving me, of making me right, just, and fair, I will know that it is all free, that it is by grace. I will spend time in praising God and building relationship with God. Not everything I do to praise and honor God will be listed on the work ethic list. I will extend that full freedom of grace to all around me. Knowing that I am saved by grace deflates any need for gossip or slander, any push to fix others, and certainly any bubbles of shame I might blow.

From what should I be saved? From extending coercion, fear, shame, and guilt to all around me and all my descendants. If I fail to submit to God's righteousness, this is where I will go, and the principle of saving myself will spread and grow in my world. If not checked, it will one day be its own pandemic.

Paul was writing about his own people, his own nation. He remembered how the leaders of his nation killed Jesus, the one who could have saved them. This is that to which their rejection of his salvation had led. Paul's heart broke for them.

Can People Who Rejected Being Saved Be Saved?

Paul wondered in writing, "Has God rejected his people?" He answered himself with a resounding "By no means! I myself am an Israelite, a descendant of Abraham" (Rom 11:1). He recalled how Elijah interceded for his people and God heard him. God told Elijah he had some people left for himself. Paul seemed sure that God had many individuals left in Israel who were chosen by grace. There were many who had submitted to God's righteousness. There were many who lived by grace and not by works according to their society's standards of doing (1 Kgs 19:10, 18).

Paul warned against being a snob like Jonah. Perhaps you were able to submit to the righteousness of God, and another person could not do that. That person rejected being saved. Later then, suppose that person has an experience that opens him or her to being saved. Paul wants you and me to be gracious and humble to all those God might be ready to graft back into himself beside you or me. We are talking about being against anti-Semitism, or any kind of racism or human phobism. When we are saved by grace, it is the inevitable result that we offer grace to others. Jonah was called to offer grace.

Paul pulled it all down to this: "All who are led by the Spirit of God are children of God. . . . and if children, then heirs, heirs of God and joint heirs with Christ" (Rom 8:14–17). This compares to his earlier statement to the Galatians, "In Christ Jesus you are all children of God through faith. . . . And if you belong to Christ, then you are Abraham's offspring, heirs according to the promise" (Gal 3:26–29). Carrying the logic out, Paul could also write, "All Israel will be saved" (Rom 11:26), both Jews and those who are not Jews, both the privileged and the marginalized (Rom 2:9–10; 3:9, 29; 9:24; 10:12; 15:8–9), all who belong to Christ.

John Perkins was called to offer grace to both the privileged and the marginalized. Born in the south to a sharecropper family in the 1930s, he has lived through and spoken God's grace amid all sorts of tumult since then. Dr. Perkins writes and speaks on "issues of reconciliation, leadership, and community development."[13] He and Karen Waddles wrote his manifesto, his legacy, in his book, *One Blood*.

Perkins and Waddles wrote:

> Our sins against our brothers and sisters are ultimately against our Father in heaven. . . and we must become broken about it."[14] "His [God's] grand vision is for each of us to be so motivated by His love that we make it our mission to be one with every other believer in Jesus Christ."[15]
>
> His [God's] will is for one Church that crosses ethnic, cultural, and class lines and is focused on bringing Him glory until He returns to redeem His bride. This picture of the church is what must fuel our prayers.

13. Perkins and Waddles, *One Blood*, cover.
14. Perkins and Waddles, *One Blood*, 80.
15. Perkins and Waddles, *One Blood*, 145.

We've got to ask Him to move everything that stands in the way of His will being accomplished. . . . I've heard it said that we should regularly pray prayers that are so big that only God could accomplish them. I believe that. And we shouldn't be afraid to ask God to do the impossible, because we know His record.[16]

Paul's Appeal

We have surveyed Rom 9, 10, and 11. Now we will read Paul's appeal in Rom 12:

> I appeal to you therefore, brothers and sisters, by the mercies of God, to present your bodies as a living sacrifice, holy and acceptable to God, which is your spiritual worship. Do not be conformed to this world, but be transformed by the renewing of your minds, so that you may discern what is the will of God—what is good and acceptable and perfect. For by the grace given to me I say to everyone among you not to think of yourself more highly than you ought to think, but to think with sober judgment, each according to the measure of faith that God has assigned. . . . Live in harmony with one another; do not be haughty, but associate with the lowly [and give yourselves humble tasks]; do not claim to be wiser than you are. (Rom 12:1–3, 16)

Let me close then with a progression of pertinent questions:

Who can be saved? I can. You can. Anyone can, by the power of Jesus' death and resurrection.

How? By relying on Christ for right, just, and fair living.

How can I stop relying on myself or my history to be good enough? By dying with Jesus in recognizing the shortfall of all my stuff.

From what will I be saved? From the principle of saving myself and from it extending coercion, fear, shame, and guilt to all around me and to all my descendants.

---

16. Perkins and Waddles, *One Blood*, 151.

Toward what will I be saved? Toward a willingness to stop and listen, to step into the language of others, to keep up conversations with those not like me, to be a blessing to all nations as God promises and Paul confirms.

To summarize and finish these chapters on Romans, I will ask and answer, "Who can be saved?" I can. "How?" By relying on Jesus, and not myself at all, to make me a praise to God and a blessing to others.

Bibliography

Anonymous. *Alcoholics Anonymous*, 3rd ed. New York: Alcoholics Anonymous World Services, 1939, 1955, 1976.
Bailey, Kenneth E. *Jacob and the Prodigal: How Jesus Retold Israel's Story*. Downers Grove: InterVarsity, 2003.
Bapopik@AOL.com. "Coolidge Quote on Preacher & Sin: 'He Was Against It' (1925)." *Linguist List*. Listserv, Jul 16, 2004. https://listserv.linguistlist.org/pipermail/ads-l/2004-July/039280.html.
Brueggemann, Walter. *Preaching Jeremiah: Announcing God's Restorative Passion*. Minneapolis: Fortress, 2020.
Chisholm, Thomas O. "Living for Jesus." In *The Christian Life Hymnal*, edited by Eric Wyse, #492. Peabody, MA: Hendrickson, 2006.
Cook, Jerry, and Stanley C. Baldwin. *Love, Acceptance, and Forgiveness: Equipping the Church to Be Truly Christian in a Non-Christian World*. Ventura, CA: Regal, 1979.
Craddock, Fred B. *Luke*. Interpretation: A Bible Commentary for Teaching and Preaching, edited by James Luther Mays. Louisville: Westminster John Knox, 1990.
Editors of Encyclopaedia Britannica. "Romulus and Remus: Roman Mythology." *Encyclopaedia Britannica*, December 9, 2020. https://www.britannica.com/biography/Romulus-and-Remus.
Elgin, Suzette Haden. *The Gentle Art of Verbal Self-Defense*. New York: Barnes & Noble, 1980.
Fineman, Howard. *The Thirteen American Arguments: Enduring Debates That Define and Inspire Our Country*. New York: Random House, 2009.
Friedman, Edwin H. *A Failure of Nerve: Leadership in the Age of the Quick Fix*. New York: Seabury, 2007.
Goodwin, Doris Kearns. *Bully Pulpit: Theodore Roosevelt, William Howard Taft, and the Golden Age of Journalism*. New York: Simon & Schuster, 2013.

Bibliography

———. *Team of Rivals: The Political Genius of Abraham Lincoln.* New York: Simon & Schuster, 2005.

Hill, Jim. "Every One of Us Has a Gift 01–16-2021." Sermon at First Christian Church (Disciples of Christ) Marietta, Jan 16, 2022, https://www.youtube.com/watch?v=qaSd_FQbbmE.

History.com Editors. "Ancient Rome." History. https://www.history.com/topics/ancient-rome/ancient-rome.

Jane's Piano Tutorial, "Bach Two-Part Invention No. 14 Piano Tutorial," YouTube video, 4:08, November 28, 2014, YouTube video, https://www.youtube.com/watch?v=ZSawsWlpiKg.

Lewis, C. S. *Till We Have Faces: A Myth Retold.* San Diego: Harcourt Brace, 1956.

Lowry, Eugene L. *The Homiletical Plot: The Sermon as Narrative Art Form.* Atlanta: John Knox, 1980.

Murray, Andrew. *Absolute Surrender.* Chicago: Moody, 1895. https://ccel.org/ccel/m/murray/surrender/cache/surrender.pdf.

———. *Humility.* Fort Washington, PA: Christian Literature Crusade, 1997.

Perkins, John M., and Karen Waddles. *One Blood: Parting Words to the Church on Race and Love.* Chicago: Moody, 2019.

"Saved." Merriam-Webster Thesaurus. https://www.merriam-webster.com/thesaurus/saved.

Scher, Isaac. "The First COVID-19 Case Originated on November 17, according to Chinese Officials Searching for 'Patient Zero.'" *Business Insider*, March 13, 2020. https://www.businessinsider.in/science/news/the-first-covid-19-case-originated-on-november-17-according-to-chinese-officials-searching-for-patient-zero/articleshow/74616604.cms.

Scott, Bernard Brandon. *The Real Paul: Recovering His Radical Challenge.* Salem, OR: Polebridge, 2015.

Stasack, Jennifer. "The Meal That Satisfies." Wycliffe Bible Translators. *InFocus*. 2.6 (2019). https://www.wycliffe.org/Resources/Publications/Infocus/2019_InFocus_Vol-25_No-6.pdf.

"Transforming Our World: The 2030 Agenda for Sustainable Development." United Nations. https://sdgs.un.org/2030agenda.

Whittle, Daniel W. "Dying with Jesus." In *The Christian Life Hymnal*, edited by Eric Wyse, #376. Peabody, MA: Hendrickson, 2006.

Wycliffe Bible Translators. *Frontlines.* Summer 2021. https://www.wycliffe.org/Resources/Publications/frontlines/2021/summer/Frontlines_Summer_2021.pdf.

www.ingramcontent.com/pod-product-compliance
Lightning Source LLC
Chambersburg PA
CBHW070509090426
42735CB00012B/2710